MANY DOORS

TO THE

4th DIMENSION

PAULINE MELLER

A spiritual journey

Who we are and why we are here

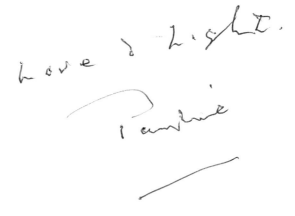

Love & Light.

Pauline

FORWARD

There is no doubt that we are living in rapidly changing times.

Everything around us is so different from even our own childhood that the 21st century promises to be like nothing mankind has experienced before. Natural disasters that plague the earth have increased in intensity, and after years of civilisation we are now faced with pollution of the oceans, overpopulation, robotic engineering, animal/human transplants, and also instant global communication, to mention but a few of our problems. All are the products of man's intelligence and ingenuity, but also evidence of his uncaring and careless attitudes where there is profit to be made, or risk of loss of power. To add to this complexity there is also no doubt that we shall soon be dealing with the wider effects of Climate Change, the extent of which has yet to be faced.

To confound matters further, into this scenario has come a Shift that began in 2012 and heralds the dawning of a new age for mankind. We are now in the Fourth Dimension where new cosmic frequencies are causing disturbances in everyone's lives and widespread conflict, disorder and unrest throughout the world.

Life on earth has always been difficult, but now it is challenging because it is so complex and stressful. For each person in the Western World it is a series of experiences some happy some difficult, but within each experience is a spiritual lesson that we need to learn for our ultimate good. It is wonderful to know that with the right motivation we can evolve from who we thought we were to understanding who we really are and why we are here. And life is but one phase after another!

CONTENTS

MANY DOORS OPEN

TALKS TO THE GROUP

MEDITATIONS

PROLOGUE

It was a lovely clear, warm, sunny day and I was feeling very regal, perched alone in the dickie seat of the high open motor car. It had been quite a scramble up the step over the rear wheel and following mother's instructions, I had been careful not to dirty my best dress. The day promised to be a happy one and I could only guess at the treats in store. To be out alone with my favourite aunt and uncle was something really special, and I loved outings in this car. There was something about the leathery smell of the upholstery and the bright, shiny brass motor horn that always excited me.

Aunt and uncle didn't have children of their own. Their nieces and nephew filled the gap and they enjoyed taking us on day trips from London through the Kentish lanes, down to Sussex and Eastbourne, Brighton or other south coast resorts, or perhaps east to Margate or Clacton. These day trips were really special, but they were usually larger family affairs. My younger sister Julia would sit between Aunt and Uncle in the front, and my parents and I would sit in the dickie with my small brother Roy on mum's lap. Now I had a new baby sister Connie, and if I thought about it at all, would have guessed that Mum was too busy with her to come along. But I was just too happy to wonder where the others were or what they were doing. It was all very exciting and I was enjoying being allowed out without them.

I suppose I was a normal eleven year old but being the eldest child a good deal was expected of me and inwardly I considered myself quite grown up. Today felt special and without the family I saw myself as really independent and quite adult. The country road down which we drove was really beautiful. Late spring flowers grew in profusion. I recognised poppies but there were other unknown yellow and blue flowers growing prettily in the hedgerows with a scattering of daisies here and there. I marvelled at the clear light and bright sunshine dappling through tall trees that gracefully bent inwards to almost form an archway over our heads. It did not strike me as strange that there was a limit to my vision. Of the surrounding countryside I could see nothing.

Suddenly we were confronted by high, black wrought iron gates such as I had only previously seen leading into a London park. But as we approached they slowly swung open to let us drive through. We were now in a lane and the sunlight had gone. It seemed then that my Aunt and Uncle became remote and removed from me. Although they were still in the car and Uncle was driving, it was as though I was alone and when I saw the first body I was unable to call out or communicate with them. They certainly did not seem to be aware of anything unusual but sat woodenly looking straight ahead.

In a flash of insight and panic, I suddenly knew why we were there. I was searching for my Mother and Father among the corpses that were now lying along the right-hand side of the lane. Anxiously I scanned the scene as Uncle drove slowly past. But there was no sign of my parents. The real horror began when, a little further on, I saw brown corpses. Naked and withered corpses, here twisted and distorted, there laid out straight and stiff, some piled high, others so entangled with each other that identification of whose limbs belonged to which head was impossible. The horror was indescribable, but I could not turn away. I had to go on searching. The responsibility for finding my parents was mine and mine alone. I did not get out of the car but sat transfixed as we motored slowly on and on. In a strange way my uncle and aunt remained uninvolved. It was as though there was a solid invisible screen between us.

I continued my fruitless search for what seemed an interminable time until it suddenly became too much to bear. In my despair, I awoke, in my own bed, trembling and frightened. Afraid to go back to sleep I lay reluctantly replaying this strange dream and in my distress found it hard to believe that my parents were in fact, asleep in the next room. It did not occur to me to wake them as their bedroom was strictly out of bounds. And so the seeds of my self-reliance and independence were sown, nurtured and consequently flourished.

But it was the beginning of a nightmare existence. By day I went to school where I was considered a bright pupil and my parents had high hopes for me. But I was lively, impatient and too easily distracted. I excelled in those subjects which interested me, but not so well where the teaching was slack and the class disruptive. It was not unknown for me to enjoy such diversions as a welcome break from what I considered to be uninteresting.

At home I was a gay, cheerful child always singing and dancing around the house and forever reading books and any scrap of print that came to hand. But essentially I was also a compliant child, the eldest and "little mother" to my sister and brother who were entrusted to my care when I came home at teatime. Discipline was strict in 1932 and we lived by predictable routines carried over from Mother's own childhood in the Edwardian period before the First World War. It was the era when we were often reminded that children were to be seen but not heard, and I was always being told to be quiet and go away and find something to do which in my case was usually reading and 'making'. Julia and I had our regular chores around the house, and meals were formal family affairs with strict observance to table manners, after which she and I would wash and dry the dishes. No dishwashers then!

Summer or winter the rule was bed at 7.30, but we would read and often talk until all light had faded from the room. But I could not confide in her or anyone else of the apprehension and dread I faced every night. Even at that age I knew without a shadow of doubt, that it would have been wrong to frighten her as I myself was afraid. My Mother was fully occupied with baby Connie, and I knew, or thought I knew, that she would have dismissed my dreams as childish nightmares and would probably have said that I was reading too much.

So it was that night after night an overwhelming and solitary dread gripped me and kept me awake until long after everyone else in the house was asleep and the summer nights had faded into darkness. Always the dream was exactly the same. The eager anticipation of an outing in the car to the countryside I loved. The joy of freedom, the sunlight playing through the branches of the trees which almost formed a tunnel overhead, and the high wide gates opening before us onto the sombre lane and the horrors beyond. The awful sight of the naked and skeletal bodies and the frantic desperate, never ending search, for my parents. The details never varied. The pressure and obligation to find them were too much for a child of eleven. But in my dream I never questioned why my Aunt and Uncle were not concerned in the search. All I knew, with utmost certainty, was that the

9

full responsibility to find them was mine. It was strange that I never travelled to the end of the lane, neither did I complete my search, before fear and distress awoke me. It was then that I lay awake tossing and turning, afraid to sleep in case it would all begin again. The nightmare in all its squalor haunted me. My thoughts often flicked back to it during the day and I dreaded bedtime. It was almost a week before I had a sound nights sleep, probably from exhaustion. From then on it became repetitive, first a few times a week, then spacing out until blessedly a few months would pass without a reoccurrence. I would grow to think that it had left me only to have a disturbing replay even after a year and then another year. Later, it took me a long time to realise that the dream had mercifully gone forever, although it lodged just under the surface of my consciousness.

In 1945, some thirteen years after the first dream, I visited a cinema with two friends and saw my first newsreel of the Allied Forces liberating a German concentration camp. And unbelievably - there was my nightmare! The dreadful details were exactly as I had seen them so many times. I could not understand what I was seeing. How could I have witnessed the bestial horrors of the extermination camps years before they had even occurred? I sat transfixed and solitary in the darkened cinema appalled, stunned and shaken by an overwhelming sense of de-ja vu.

CHAPTER 1 - SPITALFIELDS

Events happen in life which at the time seem unremarkable, but in fact, may have an extraordinary affect on our future. A casual meeting, remark or conversation may open a door leading to new employment, a new way of life, or even whole new ways of thought. There are many occasions when doors of opportunity are presented to us but we do not recognise them for what they are, or if we do, decide to pass them by. It may be that careers or personal circumstances appear at the time to be more important, and prevent us from pursuing a potentially interesting new opening. The choice is always ours and we have the freedom of action to explore or ignore that which is before us. There are times when prejudice or preconceived ideas stand between us and an open door and it should be recognised that an open mind is the surest passport of entry to an open door and all that may lie beyond.

It was such a door that opened for me in 1938 when, out of curiosity, I found myself attending a Spiritualist church. It had come about through a casual invitation from two girls who worked in the same office as myself. One had paid a previous visit to a séance which she had found interesting but so unusual that she was out of her depth and was keen to get someone else's opinion. So it was that casually and quite light heartedly, without any thought except that it might be something "different", I agreed to join them.

It was a bright spring evening when we set off for Spitalfields which at that time, was a seedy area of tenements, old houses and prostitution. In its heyday it had been the silk weaving centre of London, built round the ancient church of St Bartholomew The Great. Now its fame resided in the adjacent flourishing wholesale fruit, vegetable and flower market. The meeting was to be held in an upstairs room of one of the old buildings and the medium, Joseph Benjamin was of course, unknown to me, and anyway not yet the renowned medium he was later to become. A few years down the road it would be difficult to get into his meetings, such was his popularity and high reputation for evidential communication with the Spirit world.. At the time, and in the months that followed I did not recognise his special qualities neither did I realise how very fortunate I was to be initiated into the "ism" through such a true and gifted clairvoyant.

There were about thirty people, mainly women, already seated on wooden chairs when we arrived and were shown into a middle row. The proceedings opened with a short prayer after which the congregation sang a hymn without a piano or other musical accompaniment. Even after all these years, I never hear the lovely hymn "Nearer My God To Thee" without being transported back to relive the expectancy that was palpable in the gradually darkening room. There then followed a demonstration of clairvoyance by the medium who allegedly transmitted messages from relatives and friends who had died. The messages were pictorially detailed and appeared to be fully acceptable to the often astounded recipients.

It was unexpected, on that first evening, to be singled out by the medium who told me that I would soon be changing my job and to go ahead as it would be a very good move. This was embarrassing as my office colleagues didn't know that only a few days earlier I had taken positive steps towards obtaining a new position, and I had to make light of it and laughed it off. But secretly I was impressed! How could the medium possibly know? Was this message really from someone who was a "spirit" or might it be telepathy which seemed clever enough, or perhaps, something entirely different? Whatever, it seemed quite remarkable to me and I knew that I was being presented with a door I wanted to push open and explore.

When I got home and told Mother about the intriguing events of the evening, she confounded me by saying that my uncle, her brother Jack, was a practising Spiritual Healer, and although grandma knew, it was not talked about in the family. It appeared that he was longstanding member of the local church in Southend-on-Sea some thirty miles from London, and had built up a good local reputation for the success of his healing work. From the perspective that he was the jolliest of my mother's five brothers, the life and soul of any party, I came to the conclusion that Spitalfields was probably not so weird after all. After that night Mum, who was curious about the concept of life after death, accompanied me and we became regular members of the small congregation.

Most weeks, after the room had gradually darkened, Joseph Benjamin would retire to a corner of the L-shaped room, away from view of the sitters, to prepare for direct voice communication with those who had 'died'. At this time the congregation would be holding hands and quietly singing hymns, usually starting with "Open Mine Eyes", a beautiful hymn which set a tone of reverence for what was to come. Then a voice from the darkened recess would speak and someone among the congregation would recognise the voice and exclaim "That's my little girl" or perhaps "That's mother" and go forward to hold a conversation with their loved one. We were told this was made possible through the mediumship of Joseph Benjamin and the use of his vocal apparatus by spirit guides. The atmosphere was always highly charged and the grateful tears of those fortunate to have such conversations helped to persuade me that something very special was taking place. Something quite beyond my comprehension.

Whilst all this was happening away from the main part of the room, a healing session would be held where we were sitting. Two lady healers identified those whom they considered needed their help, although it was also possible to ask for healing. One occasion, without any prompting from me, a healer asked me to go forward which I readily agreed to do. For some time I had been suffering tummy pains which had been medically diagnosed as a 'grumbling appendix' and I had spent ten days in hospital on a special diet, to try and relieve it. However, this was unknown to those at the séance. The healing that night consisted of nothing more than a few light passes of the healer's hands across the lower part of my stomach and at the time, I had no sensation of anything special happening. Nevertheless, the healing was successful and I had immediate relief from the nagging discomfort I had been suffering.

I was not totally convinced that all "messages" came from loved ones who have passed on to the higher life. Some, I felt sure, although given in good faith, might have another source. It seemed to me at the time, that if something was occupying ones mind it might possibly be picked up mentally by a person with the gift of telepathy and that was something I could more easily accept. So I was somewhat confused. But some of my confusion was stilled when weeks, then months, then years passed without even a twinge of pain and I realised that I had experienced my first *personal* proof of the power of Spiritual healing. From that time on, I have never doubted its reality. I have known it to be successful not only in psychosomatic illnesses and those which are stress related, but also conditions of the bones, vital organs, eyesight and hearing, cancers and blood. It is unfortunate that sufferers often resort to spiritual healing and other natural healing techniques only as a last resort. They may accept that the medical profession can do little more for them, and yet still feel cheated if they don't find a miracle cure at the hands of unorthodox practitioners. Experience has shown that it is not within a healer's power to determine who will or will not be cured, although a healer with a powerful healing guide will always bring about a betterment in one form or another and to a lesser or greater degree.

Our experience at Spitalfields did not conflict with our religious beliefs at home where God played a natural part in our lives. We accepted the supremacy of His Will in all that we did and aspired to do. From a very early age mother taught us "You appoint and the Almighty disappoints". From this we understood that He was not being cruel or unkind but rather that He knew what was best for us and was very much involved in our lives. In hindsight I can see how this helped assuage our disappointment when something did not work out as we would have wished. But it instilled in us children a philosophical outlook and we became strong in spirit and accepted the variegations in life as normal and bearable.

Although both my parents were born Jewish and we were proud of our race and English heritage, due to my Father's unconventional free-thinking we had a liberal attitude to the customs and restrictions of orthodoxy. We abided by the moral code but shunned the limitations of dietary guidelines and I grew up ignorant of many of the rituals and customs that would have been normal in a religious Jewish household. Dad's views were unconventional and tempered by his awful experiences during his wartime service. He regarded all men as the sons of God and taught us that by prayer we had a "direct line" to the Almighty. As a regular soldier in the British Army and an Old Contemptible of the First World War, he was sympathetic to conscripted men of all armies realising they had little choice but to fight and kill each other to satisfy the men of power. His disillusionment with religion had its roots in the fact that clergy of all denominations, on both sides of the conflict, urged men into battle and the horrors of No-man's Land, assuring them that God and Right was on their side. This was difficult to reconcile with his own Jewish upbringing, the Christian ethic of love and charity, or the Peace of Allah.

Under his influence we accepted the Darwinian theory of man's physical evolution and regarded the bible as a combination of history, fables and moral teachings. It was quite commonplace for Dad and I to sit up all hours in debate and discussion. We ranged over thorny aspects of religion, politics – not surprisingly he was left of centre – and being on the threshold of new communication technology of which he was aware, he had visions of the new future, a great deal of which he blessedly lived to see come to fruition. Although we were both strong minded, he was instrumental in encouraging me to be independent in thought, value freedom of expression, and indeed, to stand as an individual for what I believed to be right.

As a typical teenager there was much confusion in my mind. There were so many questions I wanted to have answered. What, I mused, is life all about? Why are we born? Why are we here? What does it all mean? What is the purpose of it all? Why is it so important that we should always be honest and truthful, never go back on our given word, be responsible and not let other people down? I understood about trying to be kind and helpful and putting other peoples' needs before our own, but it did not answer the question of *why* we should always do what is regarded by society as being right, even though it may involve considerable inconvenience or difficulties for ourselves. I confess to wondering if it all really mattered as long as we were doing our best? It did not occur to me to ask if my best was good enough!

But through my visits to Spitalfields I came to accept that an afterlife probably existed. If true it would make some sense in light of the questions bothering me. But my Father would have none of it. He had seen too much warfare. Too many men obliterated to be able to accept that any part of them could still exist. For him death was final and in spite of our coaxing to come with us to a meeting, he was adamant in his refusal. In our opinion he was being obstinate and intolerant. In his eyes we were being gullible and naïve. It was one argument I just could not win!

15

These early experiences encouraged me to think that perhaps death was not the end and that we might continue to live after we "die". If this were so, perhaps communication between those here and those who had passed on, could actually take place. I had experienced the effectiveness of Spiritual healing and recognised that to be able to relieve pain must involve a fantastic power for good. I was inclined to think that the spirit 'messages' I had heard and experienced, probably or possibly, came from the same source. But beyond that my knowledge was limited and I knew little more than I have shown here. At that time it was sufficient for me to believe in the existence of a supreme loving power whom we called God and I felt that everything I had seen and heard at Spitalfields was part of God's work.

My knowledge and experience of personal guides and helpers and the interaction between the spirit realms and our own, did not come until many years later and then only by degrees. An account of the gradual discovery of my own psychic ability which developed parallel to an equally gradual evolvement of spiritual awareness, and has led to a measure of spiritual progression, is the theme of this book. It is written in the hope that it may help others on a similar pathway of discovery and that they may find many open doors along the way.

There are so many people whose thoughts, prompted by their deeply hidden spiritual consciousness, take them beyond the parameters of conventional religious doctrine. They often feel isolated and even a little odd, believing there are no others around to share their ideas and embryonic philosophy. They recognise that there must be more to life than the daily grind. And more to life than parties, holidays and other pleasures that are the material rewards of a material world. They may recognise that these pleasures, whilst enjoyable at the time, have little lasting value. When the holiday is over and the party finished, it is easy to slip into discontent and a yearning for something deeper. But there are thousands and thousands of others who feel the same spiritual hunger and search for a doorway to lead them into understanding that there is far more to life than appears. They have yet to realise that the unseen is more real than that which has form and substance but being material is transient and will often let us down.

CHAPTER 2 – UNWELCOME VISITOR

The beginning of the Second World War put an end to our visits to Spitalfields. Life changed for everyone over the next few years. Most of the population, certainly all the young people, were uprooted and directed into new surroundings where they met people and situations outside their normal experience and lifestyle. Millions of those in the armed forces were subjected to hardship and danger beyond their imagination, and countless others had to adapt to working in factories, coal mines and on the land. But it was not all discomfort and adversity. In those eventful times life quickened as young people realised there may not be many tomorrows and life had to be lived to the full. In the new found freedom life became exciting, friendships were easily made (some lasting a long lifetime) and love was urgent and compelling. It was the older generation who had already lived through the First World War and experienced its horrors, who were most anxious and apprehensive of wholesale slaughter, fearing the future and the wiping out of another generation of the nation's young men.

In the field of employment it had become apparent that I quickly became restless once a particular job or routine had been mastered. Backed up by a glowing school reference I was full of confidence and ever ready to explore new grounds and new challenges, and in the process of moving from job to job gained a wide appreciation and knowledge of office routines in a variety of commercial and manufacturing businesses. Even at the early age of 17 I ran the office of a manufacturing factory whilst the boss was away from Monday to Friday. My responsibilities included ensuring goods were made and despatched to those customers who would pay cash so that I could meet the demands of promissory notes that I stuck on the wall above my desk! And I made a fortune for another company who were the last to have genuine sandbags for sale in London, all of which set me thinking that at some time in the future I should be working for myself.

Then our home in London fell casualty to the bombing and the family unexpectedly found itself living in Gloucestershire. For almost a year I ran the library in a local W.H. Smith bookshop, and then Julia and I obtained employment in the offices of a shadow factory making guidance instruments for the R.A.F. This was classified as essential work and meant we were safe from being conscripted into the armed forces, Land Army or making munitions. But it was the attraction of doing something adventurous that persuaded us to leave our safe "reserved" occupations and volunteer to join the Auxiliary Territorial Service (A.T.S.) – the women's army in which we served for almost four years back in the London area.

Julia and I worked in the battery offices of heavy anti-aircraft sites, she in the accounts and general office and myself undertaking the postings and documentation of personnel who were sent on courses or leave, or who were hospitalised and then moved to other units. Eventually our paths split and for a brief spell I found myself with the battery of anti-aircraft guns in Hyde Park. It was a show site for visiting Royalty and VIPs and it was quite peculiar that there were always members of the public standing with their noses pressed against our wire perimeter fence watching us (boys and girls) drilling and changing guard each evening. It was also where Winston Churchill's daughter Mary (later Lady Soames) was in the adjoining office. She was a charming subaltern and luckily for us, very generous with sharing the boxes of chocolates she brought in from her many admirers.

Word came that I had been selected to go on special duties involving top secret work and promotion - an exciting prospect. When it materialised I found myself among a group of people forming a new army headquarters at a secret location in west London. But it was not quite straightforward and for a month I lazed away the time on the cricket pitch working up a good suntan in the wonderful spring of 1943. They did not quite know what to do with me and after a spell in Intelligence (which was boring) I found myself temporarily sharing an office with a very quiet young draughtsman who was engrossed in his work preparing signals communications for the coming invasion of Europe. He barely seemed to notice me but I could not fail to notice him. His natural grace, reserve and good manners were in contrast to the general ruggedness I had met in so many other young men. Ron's refinement set him apart, and when we eventually talked I found in him a maturity and wisdom far beyond his twenty-two years. I felt drawn to him and instinctively felt he was someone I could trust, someone who would be reliable and upon whom I could depend. We started going out and about with a small group of friends and they were all charmed and amused by his sharp wit and good humour. At that time in London there were several sources of free theatre tickets for troops, and on our days off Ron and I took full advantage of what was on offer and saw most of the shows and films currently on in the West End. And I taught him to dance. He was graceful and stylish and ball-room dancing became our favourite past-time for the next fifty-four years.

It was a whirlwind courtship which confounded our friends who thought we were too dissimilar to find lasting happiness. In many ways we were opposites who complemented each other. Quick and slow, impetuous and thoughtful, extravagance and caution, and where I would act on intuition or experience he required time, sometimes days, to consider facts. When in later years I asked him why he had married me, he replied quite simply, "Because I saw the good in you." At the time it seemed an ambiguous reply and it took half a lifetime for me to understand that we had recognised each other on a spiritual level above normal consciousness. We had a war-time wedding in the registrar office in Stroud with our families some eight months after we first met and just before the army sent him to Europe. In the meantime I had become part of the Commander-in-Chief's small personal staff and felt that I was doing a good job and enjoying doing it.

I take up my story again in 1945 when after demobilisation I went to Birmingham to live with my mother-in-law and await Ron's return to this country from Belgium and his longed for release after more than 6 years in the army. It was a time of high hopes and anticipation when every ex-serviceman and woman was looking forward to making a new life. In my case the immediate reality was quite different from what I had anticipated. I had only met my mother-in-law twice before getting married and quite unexpectedly, and without prior warning from Ron, I found myself living with a sad, neurotic woman whose sole mind-set and preoccupation was her husband's desertion some eleven or twelve years earlier and the resulting divorce. She had no other interest and it was still her main, and almost only, topic of conversation, so that she was completely unable to get on with her life. In her misery she had allowed herself to be eaten up by bitterness and recriminations. Today, there no longer being stigma attached to divorce, she would have been able to receive sympathetic counselling through the medical profession and various agencies. Or perhaps, she may have allowed herself to be helped by spiritual healing or a therapy that could have induced a calmer state of mind. And no doubt, during healing sessions she would have received counselling encouraging her to open her heart and mind to forgiveness and release the bitterness that ruled her. But she was isolated in her unhappiness.

I was not a patient person at the best of times and I can honestly say that I tried to cope, although the situation was quite alien to me. Despite the fact that I had worked in the West End of London from a very early age and met some very odd people, and I had spent years in the army, it was the first time in my life that I had faced such a negative attitude. My home life had been strict but it was loving and although we might mildly argue and bicker as in most families, it was without rancour or malice and I had no experience of antagonism or bitterness. To my consternation I discovered that her antagonism even extended to me, as I was seen as the person who had come between her and her dreams for the future which had been built around Ron, her only son who remained at home. The interminable harping on one subject and the constant tears affected me so that I felt trapped in a situation beyond my control. After a few months it came to the point when it was more than I could handle and I fled.

At the time I did not have the awareness to understand that under spirit influence I was being guided out of a depressing and negative situation which could have adversely affected my very being. It was only much later when I learned that we are what we think, and that our thoughts today fashion the person we become tomorrow, that I realised how right it had been for me to leave. This episode and the one that immediately followed, proved to be important staging posts along my life's pathway, and were the first intimation I had that bad times and experiences often lead to unimaginable good fortune and happiness.

My father-in-law was a totally different person from his ex-wife and doubtless my parents-in-law had been an ill matched couple. He was a tall, slim, refined and educated man, softly voiced with a kind, gentle nature. In fact, he was an older version of my husband and it was not difficult to turn to him for help. I had found a couple of rooms in a private house that was not entirely to my liking, so I 'phoned him and was invited out to dinner to talk things over. In the quiet atmosphere of a small restaurant in the centre of Birmingham he listened sympathetically to my situation, and I appreciated that he was the one person who could really understand the conditions I had fled from.

Although naturally reserved and cautious and not given to extravagant gestures, he nevertheless came to my rescue by kindly offering to let me live in his Birmingham town house whilst he was living in the countryside of Droitwich with his present wife. It was a wonderful solution to my problems and I gratefully accepted on the basis that I would move out when they wished to move back to town. Which was how I found myself occupying a half furnished, nine roomed, three storey house in South Yardley. The fact that the house was cold and sombre was not surprising as it had stood virtually empty most of the war years. But I chose to ignore the disadvantages as it was a relief to be alone and away from the depleting environment of recent months.

Across the top of the house was a large billiard room, whilst in the basement was an extensive cellar. On the floors between were four bedrooms two of which were unfurnished, and on the ground floor a sitting room, dining room, study and kitchen, all linked by three flights of stairs. The longest flight led from the ground floor to the first and was situated so that when ascending one's back was turned to the door of the billiard room above. It was always unnerving to go up to bedrooms on the first floor as it was impossible to escape the uncanny feeling of being observed by someone standing in the doorway above. The stare seemed to penetrate and prickle the back of my head, but when I turned to look up there was never anyone there. Only once I climbed the short top flight and ventured into the room where I found a billiard table, chairs and various storage boxes, but it was icy cold and I wasn't brave enough to stay.

After moving into my new accommodation I made it a priority to find permanent employment that would lead to a fulfilling career. I had several offers locally, but eventually accepted a post on the other side of town. In addition to private secretarial duties to the Personnel Manager, I was employed as Welfare and Personnel Officer for the female staff of a group of five small engineering companies all under one roof. It was a responsible interesting job with no two days alike, and there was no doubt that I had found my ideal occupation. A bonus came in the form of two wonderful new friendships. Rita was a director's private secretary and Norma was chief cook in charge of the group's canteens and although I saw more of Rita as she lived near to me, Norma and I also had a great deal in common as she too, had served in the A.T.S. and we sometimes visited each other at the weekend or went into the town centre to do shopping.

There was one particular evening when Rita and I went to see the latest Hollywood film and the programme unexpectedly included a newsreel of the liberation of a concentration camp by our troops. The horror and revulsion that was shared by all who saw it was, in my case, compounded by the fact that I had seen those same piles of brown withered bodies laid out in the same manner, many, many times before. I sat there stunned and speechless, washed over by so many emotions of which incredulity was paramount. How could I have seen the events – and in such detail – so many years before they had happened? Or when had they happened, and was I dreaming again? I went home troubled and confused not knowing what to make of it. I had no answers although I eventually came to question whether there might be a connection between my experience, and the predictions into the future given by Joseph Benjamin at Spitalfields.

Housing was a difficult problem after the war. Bombing had taken its toll, women had often returned to their parental home and no new housing had been built. The little accommodation there was available commanded high rents and it was the practise for landlords to take advantage of the situation and insist that prospective tenants purchase inferior carpets, second-hand armchairs and other bits and pieces of furniture. In this way the property acquired legal status as furnished accommodation that gave favourable terms to the landlord. At the same time they were charging premiums for keys to the property. Moving was an expensive and frustrating business, often beyond the pockets of ex-service personnel. So although I knew my new accommodation was temporary and not a long term solution, I was very grateful to my father-in-law for giving me a rent free home.

It became normal for him to come to the house twice a week to pick up his mail and take me into town for dinner. They were pleasant evenings which I looked forward to, and I am sure it pleased him to have a young, attractive girl on his arm. In short, we enjoyed each others company. The house however, continued to feel chilly, even unwelcoming. It needed to be fully furnished and warmth brought into its walls. It needed a family to live in it and laugh in it. As it was, I found it difficult to be really comfortable and when I went out with my father-in-law or friends, I contrived to return as late as possible before settling down to write my daily letter to Ron, and then it would be time for bed.

It was one night, some months after my arrival, when I had written my letter and was just settling down to sleep in my first floor bedroom, that I heard footsteps coming up the stairs. There were various creaks and sounds in the old house but there was no mistaking the fact that these *were* footsteps. Immediately I was alert and anxious. Listening intently I sensed the bedroom door opening – but there was no sound. In the eerie silence I half lifted my head and peered towards the foot of the bed. My heart pounded in my throat as there in the dim light from the window stood a figure. It was impossible to distinguish if it was a man or woman, but that was not important, as I knew it was not a real person as it had a flimsy, opaque quality and no visible features.

My recollection of Spitalfields came to the rescue. Without much confidence, but feeling the situation called for some kind of action, I whispered, "Who are you? What do you want?" There was no reply and the figure just melted away. I knew I had not been dreaming – I had not been to sleep! Whatever had happened was for real!

The next day I reflected on the night's events and found I wasn't really too upset, although I could not claim to be overjoyed either. I accepted that a house could be haunted, but everything at Spitalfields had been presented in such a natural and friendly way that I didn't feel threatened by my ghostly visitor. It was sure to be an isolated event, at least I hoped so, as I had no wish for such experiences. However, my hopes were soon dashed and I became really disturbed when visitations reoccurred on a regular basis. Sometimes two or three nights in a row I heard footsteps on the stairs and sensed the door opening after which the presence would go down the side of the bed and stand at the bottom looking at me. I somehow came to the conclusion that my unwelcome visitor was a man and there were times when I would speak and ask why he had come, or bless him and ask him to go away. At other times it was all too much and I shrank down in the big double bed, keeping my head firmly under the bedclothes until I instinctively knew that he had left.

The climax came one night when I heard footsteps on the stairs and waited for him to enter in his usual way. Instead the door was forcibly flung open and I felt a cold draught as the bedclothes were thrown back behind me and then, incredibly, the bed sank under the weight of someone getting in beside me. There was no sound or word. I held my breath - could this really be happening? A cold tension gripped me and I was absolutely terrified! My first thought was that the house had been broken into and this was an intruder or burglar. My second thought was that a well aimed knee to his crotch would be my best defence. So I hurled myself round – but there was no-one there!

I had had enough! I decided then and there that I needed to confide in someone, and in spite of, or perhaps because of, his practical but kindly manner, I decided to talk to my father-in-law about it. It was difficult to gauge what his reaction might be. My mind went over and over what had happened and I pondered on how I was going to tell him something so outlandish. It would probably be difficult to convince him that such events had really taken place and it was practical to expect him to say that such things were not possible. Afterwards I would have to leave the house. Having prepared and steeled myself for the ordeal, it was with almost disbelief that I heard him apologising for not letting me know that his wife's father still roamed the house and that she had seen him on several occasions! He had not wanted to alarm me and out of consideration for my feelings and peace of mind had not told me of previous disturbances. Neither had he told me that I was sleeping in the old man's bed!

At his suggestion I confided in Rita and Norma who, knowing me to be practical and level headed in business, did not question the truth of the matter and accepted the situation in true friendship. The outcome was that all three joined forces to ensure that in future I did not sleep in the house alone. And strangely whilst they were there I was not aware of any further disturbances. It was as though the old man had made his point – I was trespassing in his bed and he wanted me to know it. Or, more likely, he wanted me out of it.

A sequel occurred sometime later when my sister Julia and her husband came to visit for a few days whilst he was being demobilised from the army at a nearby camp. The day after they arrived was his big day and being a conscientious hostess, I got up and cooked him breakfast. It was about 6.30 on a cold November morning when he left the house, far too early to start the day, so pouring myself a cup of tea I returned to the bed settee in the sitting room where I had spent the night.

At about 8.30 I made more tea and took a cup upstairs to my bedroom where Julia and her husband had slept. She opened her eyes and thanking me for the tea, laughed mischievously.

"I fooled you", she said.

"Did you? How?"

"When you came in earlier. I kept my eyes closed."

"What do you mean ….. when I came in earlier?"

"Well, you know. You came in softly and walked to the bottom of the bed, but I

kept my eyes closed. I didn't want to get up so early." Wow! That was a shock!

Shortly afterwards my father-in-law and his wife moved back into the house and then Ron came back from India and was demobilised from the army, and many doors opened as we began a new and eventful life together.

CHAPTER 3 – ENTER PETER

By the mid-1950's we were happily settled in the small, prosperous town of Redditch set in the beautiful countryside of south Worcestershire. We now had a young daughter Jose', and to supplement our income I had started a small business operating from home. Ron meanwhile, was studying and working hard in design engineering trying and make up for almost seven years he had lost to the army. And there was a lot of catching up to do. In common with many other young men, he had returned from the forces to find he was regarded as little more than a junior and was striving to prove his worth.

From time to time thoughts of my psychic experiences would come to mind, but always with a sense of isolation as I knew of no-one with a similar interest. It was maddening that Ron was so sceptical. He could not reconcile the ghostly visitations at his father's house with our own survival after death and ridiculed my ideas and beliefs. Strangely however, he always asserted that he was not afraid of death. As young lad he had had the unusual experience of hearing a doctor pronounce him dead whilst acutely ill in hospital with pneumonia. It was a vivid memory that stayed with him all his life and to which he often referred, saying, "There is nothing to fear. Dying is nothing more than sliding into a deep sleep."

It is not uncommon among men to be reluctant to acknowledge the existence of psychic phenomena or a spirit world unless certain criteria can be met to their personal satisfaction. Some need it to be explained in terms of the five physical senses or scientifically demonstrated repeatedly under laboratory conditions. Others require it to conform to their understanding of logic. At the root of this reluctance is often the fear of being thought foolish or gullible. I have found however, that when a man accepts that there is an ethereal world he is usually steadfast in his belief as he will have arrived at his conclusion by means which will have satisfied his personal reasoning. On the whole women, being more intuitive, find it easier to accept the *possibility* of an afterlife and a spirit world, and are likely to want to know more.

It is unfortunate that preconditioning by religious doctrine often creates a barrier that prevents both sexes from accepting the possible reality of a spirit world that interpenetrates with our own. This is in spite of the fact that both the New and Old Testaments of the bible are full of psychic happenings, guidance by angels, miraculous healing and intervention by God in human affairs.

We were quite unaware of how our lives were to be turned upside down when we casually met John and Pam over a cup of tea at a mutual friend's house. They were an extremely attractive couple. She was an exhibition ballroom dancer, tall and stately with her pale, blonde hair piled high on her head. She was lovely and very sociable, whilst he had wit, boyish good looks and impeccable manners which added to his charm. They were slightly younger than us, recently married and as we were all mad about dancing and socialising, we came to see a lot of each other. We thought we knew them well, but one evening, relaxing in our sitting room, John announced that his parents Mary and George, were moving up from London and would be living near us in the town. And, out of the blue, he confided that they were a family of Spiritualists!

When he was only six years old an uncle had taken Peter along to a Spiritualist church meeting. The impact of the people he met and what he heard and saw at the meeting instilled in him an unusual curiosity for one so young. He badgered his parents to allow him to attend a lyceum – the Spiritualist church's equivalent to a C. of E. Sunday school, and he progressed from there to being a church member. In his early twenties he wondered whether he had been blinkered by having such an early introduction to this particular philosophy and ceased to go to the church. But he could not escape from his true pathway, and a little later his business career began to take him all over the world including the Far East, Nepal, India and the Middle East, America and Africa. During these journeys he met and spoke with people of other religious persuasions and his beliefs turned a full circle and brought him back to the firm conviction that "Spiritualism is the most inclusive of all religions".

A newspaper article written many years later when he became a town councillor quoted him as saying, "After I had met many different religious people I began to realise that the basic universal law at the root of all religions was eternity, spirituality and the fact that man progresses according to how he lives his lives." He went on to say that Spiritualists believe in one universal God and one universal set of natural and spiritual laws that govern all creation in whatever dimension it may be.

"Whereas other religions say you will believe this because I say so, or this book says so," he said, "this has not happened in Spiritualism. We say instead that you will experience this for yourself. Spiritualists will give guide lines, but at the end of the day, only your own experience will convince you whether there is a God and an afterlife or not."

He added the warning that seances and ouija boards have no place in modern Spiritualism without proper supervision "It could be very dangerous to someone highly sensitive," he asserted, "like a novice flying an aeroplane without a qualified pilot".

By the time we met he had already visited the Far East and Nepal and had been impressed by the people he had met. He had not the slightest doubt that what we call death is but the gateway to a new form of existence on a higher plane of life.

He had no hesitation in declaring, "As far as my consciousness is concerned, it is perfectly natural to communicate with people from the spirit world." Pam was tolerant but not at all convinced and both she and Ron soon tired of listening to our discussions which often went on quite late, until the particular night Ron went out of the room and came back in his pyjamas! Enough said!

To me John was like a breath of fresh air. Not only was he sympathetic to my psychic experiences, but he answered many of the questions generated by events at Spitalfields and at my father-in-law's house. My talks with him confirmed my belief that we have existed before and will continue to exist after so-called death. This present lifetime is only one very small part of our eternal existence and may be likened to a passage with a door at either end through which we must all travel, coming from one dimension of consciousness through to another.

John came into our lives at exactly the right time. Not that I had been entirely idle up to meeting him as it troubled me to know how, as a child, I had been able to see into the future. And did it happen to everyone, and if not, why me? My search had led me to Dunne's theory that Time is the fourth dimension of infinitive space. In this concept Time may be visualised as being laid out like a road. A road we are required to travel and where we are destined to meet certain experiences. With my lack of scientific education I did not find it an easy theory to follow, certainly not the mathematics that accompanied it, but it propounded a degree of fatalism that, at the time, had a certain appeal.

It suggested that if certain events are already in existence in an unknown (he called it 'fourth') dimension of Time, then there is probably a natural explanation of how events may be seen ahead of our normal time scale. But I did not have any idea of how that could be accessed even though I had experienced doing so.

Through discussions with Peter I came to recognise the importance of the Spiritualist principle of Personal Responsibility for all our thoughts and actions. If one accepts the Fourth Dimension and the theory of Predestination where certain events are preordained, how, I wondered, can this be equated with Personal Responsibility? And where does Precognition fit in? In simplistic terms, my understanding at that time was that there is a Divine Plan for the world and within that plan is a pathway for each individual soul. No pathway is in isolation, but interacts with all others along the way. Along each plan and pathway there are certain experiences we are destined to meet, but there will always be choices and the opportunity to exercise personal free will through the many possibilities that present themselves.

Perhaps this may be illustrated by visualising several interacting circumstances, which being in motion are following their prescribed courses. If there are no deviations it should be possible to give an educated guess of an outcome, or even an accurate forecast. It is possible that the spirit realms, being in a different dimension, not subject to the limitations of our earthly time scale, have a wider overall view of our pathway and are able to correctly forecast events which lie in the future.

I visualised that the situation may be similar to a traffic controller in a police helicopter who has an overall view of a motorway. He can see traffic congestion building up ahead and is able to direct traffic so that they may take avoiding action. Likewise he may see that if the pattern of certain erratic or dangerous driving is sustained, an accident is certain to occur and he may be able to pinpoint the exact place it will happen. Within these and similar circumstances drivers have personal responsibility and choice of action. They may heed police advice and leave the motorway to avoid congestion, or take warning and change their mode of driving, or conceivably, they may disregard advice and warnings and choose to continue as before with predictable results.

This hypothesis gave me some measure of understanding and satisfaction at the time, although it must be appreciated that I was using my limited human intelligence and applying reason with my finite mind. Although it is pleasing to arrive at an explanation that satisfies the intellect, it is often the intellect itself which forms a barrier to greater understanding. Matters of the spirit are more likely to be understood intuitively through a deeper consciousness than by rational thinking or thoughts generated by our Ego. This deeper consciousness will be discussed later as I gradually became aware of its complex nature.

From time to time I have had other experiences of precognition during sleep state and have found that they have fallen into three categories. A few have been similar to the preview of the extermination camp; events that are far into the future and appear to serve me no purpose. Among those was the funeral of Gamal Abdul Nasser the Egyptian President who was assassinated in 1970, and again the newsreels were identical to my dream. Another that took years to come to fruition involved hundreds of pilgrims to Mecca who were trapped in a fire disaster. This last vision was foretold to our group at the time I saw it, but as I say, doesn't appear to have served me any purpose to have seen it, but doubtless I had crossed a time zone.

Other instances of precognition have drawn me to the conclusion that the veil is drawn aside when it will be helpful to me, such as the time when in a "dream" I saw my parents and other members of my family standing round a freshly dug grave. They were not sad, in fact I noted they were relaxed and smiling. I peered down into the grave which was lined with artificial grass, and found it empty! The tricky part is, of course, the interpretation! My conclusion was that someone in the family was going to be very ill but that it would not be fatal. The one person missing from the graveside was my sister Julia and I thought that if I told her that *someone* was going to be ill but that it would not be fatal, it would be helpful to her if she were to be the victim. I also told my parents to be prepared for a family illness. In the event, within a month, my Dad had a heart attack, the first of several. It was a significant as it marked the beginning of twelve years for him as a semi-invalid. My vision was a blessing for the family, who were spared a great deal of worry and anxiety in the knowledge that he was going to pull through that first attack.

The third category of precognition comes into play when I am trying to help others through healing or counselling. Often a glimpse into the future proves valuable to the recipient, but I believe it is more useful is a look into the past to find the underlying cause of an existing health problem but both can become part of a healing process.

CHAPTER 4 – NEW BEGINNINGS

Peter and I often regretted the fact that there were no other people around with similar interests to our own, except of course his parents Harry and Phyllis who had helped to run churches in London and Paignton in Devon. We were quite unaware that for several years a small group had been holding weekly Spiritualist meetings in a house on the far side of town. It therefore came out of the blue to see an advertisement for the proposed formation of a Spiritualist church in town. We could not begin to speculate who might be behind it, but were naturally interested and very curious to know more. Although I could not have persuaded Ron to attend the meeting our discussions must have had some affect because he volunteered to come with Peter, Pam and me to see what it was all about. Luckily, suspecting this might happen I had already bought him a ticket.

This occurred in 1963 not long after I had put to good use my wide experience of office systems, recruitment and personnel, and had opened offices as a recruitment consultant. I was now well known in town and not knowing who the organisers were it seemed wise that we should not sit as a group, but split up so as not to hint at our relationships.

The inaugural meeting had attracted a large number of people and when we arrived the hall was getting full. We had not known what to expect and were delighted to find that the President of the Spiritualists National Union was to give the address. Gordon Higginson, a natural psychic from childhood, had been rigorously trained to be a platform demonstrator by his mother, herself a medium. Much to his chagrin she barred him from appearing in churches and demonstrating in public until he had developed his gifts to an outstanding level of competence. It is to her credit that she ensured that he would not be content with demonstrating anything less that than the highest possible evidence of survival and spiritual guidance. This had meant long patient years of meditation and study, until he achieved close communication with his guides in the spirit world and was confident that the messages and information he relayed would be reliable and accurate. He was a man of exceptional psychic ability and the channel for detailed, evidential messages that were intimate and meaningful to those who received them. He often amazed audiences by including in his messages full identification with surnames, place names and driving licence numbers etc.

The meeting that evening heard of his early beginnings and he then went on to explain that in 1958 modern Spiritualism had become recognised as a religion with the same legal standing as any other religion. Their Ministers are able to conduct marriages, funerals and naming ceremonies etc. Gordon explained that members are asked to recognise Seven Principles on which the philosophy of Spiritualism is based, and listed them as The Fatherhood of God, The Brotherhood of Man, The Communion of Spirits and the Ministry of Angels, The Continuous Existence of the Human Soul, Personal Responsibility, Compensation and Retribution Hereafter for all the good and evil deeds done on earth, and finally, Eternal Progress open to every human soul.

He told his rapt audience that given the right conditions, Spiritualism seeks to prove what all other religions preach – continuation of life after death. He explained that when we die we shed our earthly outer body and release our spirit into a new dimension – a plane of existence that operates on finer vibrations and frequencies than those of the earth plane. What we call death is but a natural rebirth and how we conduct our lives here will determine our spiritual status in the afterlife.

So many people are instinctively aware that there is more to life than appears on the surface. Life should mean more than working, taking holidays and leading a purely materialistic way of living. He asserted that awareness of an afterlife, proven through communication with those who have passed on, could change the lives of those present and give them a spiritual purpose for living. He urged his audience not to accept his word, but investigate for themselves with an open mind, and he had no doubt that their lives would become happier and more contented. Most impressive stuff!

I had been surprised to see Nancy, a friend who owned a manufacturing company, taking an active role among the organisers of the meeting as I had no idea that she was interested in such matters. But it was she who telephoned me the following morning to ask whom I thought might be President of the newly formed church and I had no hesitation in recommending Peter. He readily agreed, and with George as Secretary we quickly got off the ground by hiring a room in a public building for weekly meetings.

At that time in the early nineteen-sixties, there were many mature and dedicated mediums serving churches in the south Midlands. They had been operating since before the church had gained statutory respectability and all were eager to offer guidance and help to get us off the ground. Additionally, they freely gave their time and demonstrated their excellent mediumship. It was apparent from the outset that they were drawn to Ron, as week after week various demonstrators singled him out as a potential powerful healer. They would see him surrounded by an aura of the deepest, clearest blue which signifies healing energy, and repeatedly urged him to allow himself to be used as a channel for Spiritual healing. But being naturally reticent, he was most reluctant to put it to the test, and chose to ignore the door that was being held open for him.

As a new church it was obviously desirable to establish a core of people at least as informed and developed as Peter and his parents. To this end a development circle was formed under the guidance of a long established medium from the Midlands. It was important to begin in this way because any group sitting together for the purpose of communicating with the spirit world should ensure that they are under the direction of an experienced medium who has the help and protection of her own (known) highly evolved guides and helpers. To do otherwise would be similar to opening the front and back doors of ones home and allowing any stranger to enter or pass through.

When people pass into the next world they are not transformed into superior beings, but take with them their intelligence and spiritual understanding which will include their prejudices and attitudes. Those who demonstrated anti-social behaviour in their earthly lifetime will continue in the same frame of mind. Others, because of the nature of their passing, may be consumed with hatred against their fellow men and seek revenge by creating mischief or influencing others to commit evil. It is possible that they may attach themselves to a particular person and those playing with

34

ouija boards for fun, or are experimenting by sitting in an unprotected circle without an experienced medium in charge, are easy targets.

When we embarked on our circle work we didn't know our own guides and placed ourselves under the guardianship of the experienced medium's guides in good faith that no undesirable entity would be allowed to infringe our circle, and no intrusion ever took place. Some call these particular guides "door-keepers" as their function is to protect and not allow unwelcome spirits to influence us.

John and Pam kindly let us meet once a week at their house and we began to build up the right conditions for our own personal guides to make themselves known. Gradually most of us realised that we were developing clairvoyance. It was a slow process of visualisation and impressions and, importantly, learning to interpret what we were seeing and feeling. Only one sitter proved to be clairaudient, although others might be impressed by words or sentences. We were a happy group, united by common purpose that was that we all wished to work towards a successful, established church and aspired to form a healing clinic. It was this unified motivation that made us so compatible and we made steady progress including Ron whose meditation was deep but otherwise unremarkable.

The psychic gifts that enable a medium to become a channel by which messages can be conveyed from the spirit world are categorised as clairvoyance (clear seeing), clairaudience (clear hearing) and clairsentience (mental impression). These three gifts provide the most satisfactory channels by which accurate evidence may be obtained. Healing is a separate channel working on a different vibration and as will be seen, may work in conjunction with any or all of the other three. However, possession of these gifts is without value unless the medium, can correctly interpret that which spirit is trying to transmit without adding her own thoughts and impressions to the message. Hence the years of training it takes to be really competent.

After joining a circle and learning to relax and meditate, it is often possible to assist psychic development by practising automatic writing or psychometry. But this was quite unknown to me until one evening after a church service when I was thanking the visiting medium for her excellent service. She clasped my hand in both of hers and asked. "Do you do psychometry?"

"No" I vaguely replied, not really understanding what she meant.

She smiled, "My dear, you will. Before my next visit. You'll see."

I had no idea what I was expected to do until I read that it is possible to hold an article, say a piece of jewellery, and obtain impressions of the previous owner. It has long been known that people leave their imprint in their surroundings or on objects they have habitually worn or handled. Objects absorb the essence of their owners and often the circumstances and surroundings in which they existed. Impressions seem to vary in strength and some ancient buildings seem to harbour within their walls atmospheric conditions many decades or centuries after particularly disagreeable events. Additionally, places and events connected with a person's past may be seen by the handler's inward clairvoyant eye. It is not unknown for sensitive people to find they are unable to wear second-hand jewellery that in the past has absorbed sad events, or to have in their homes pieces of antique pottery or metal which appear to radiate sadness or ill-ease into the house. These moods could transfer to the new owner and it follows that it is unwise for persons of a nervous disposition to attempt psychometry. However, this skill can be useful for developing psychic ability.

The visiting medium's prophecy seemed a tall order, but never one to avoid a challenge, I was soon wearing the patience of friends by taking ages to produce even the smallest shred of evidence. I find the best material for me to use is metal and it is essential that the article should have been owned by only one person. When more than one person has owned say, a ring or watch, results can be confusing. It took a great deal of practice before I was able to produce good clairvoyant pictures in full colour and interpret them in a way that was meaningful to the sitter. It is particularly satisfying to both parties when I have not met the sitter before, or know very little about him or her.

There are many examples of highly developed psychometric mediums who are consulted by the police in cases of missing persons and these are well documented. But I had not been practising long when one of our helpers in the church, Viv, told me she had lost her diamond ring and asked if I could find it. I sat in a quiet room and asked to be helped and shown where the ring was. I had not previously been to her house but I saw a room with dark, heavy furniture and my attention was directed to a thick blue curtain that hung on a rod fixed to the back of the door. My eye travelled down the curtain and there behind the door, in the corner entangled in the folds of the curtain, was the missing ring. Viv and I were both thrilled and this lovely success gave me the encouragement to keep practising.

It was not long after this that I got a phone call from Nancy who asked if I could help her find a contract of employment in respect of her Sales Manager with whom she was having problems. I had not been to her factory and had no idea of her set-up, but again I sat quietly and asked to be shown its whereabouts. I was trying to keep an open mind and not expect to see a particular filing cabinet somewhere. And then what I actually saw was a couple of box files on a dusty window ledge of what might have been a very small room. But I didn't see the room, instead my focus was on one box that I knew held the missing contract. And so it proved to be.

I was still at what I considered to be the experimental stage of psychometry when a young junior typist in my office enquired if I thought I could get results from an earring. She was a quiet, reserved girl who had been with us only a short time but she obviously had been chatting with other members of staff, all of whom knew of my weird interest in the paranormal. I agreed to see her in a lunch break and we settled down in two chairs facing each other. Holding the earring in my closed fist, I got an immediate, clear picture of a dark, good looking young woman in a grey silk dress that had a cross-over bodice. She wore earrings. She looked fully at me and smiled and as she did so I felt a warm wave of love and affection sweep over me that I knew was for my sitter. She was standing on a footpath in front of a grey brick house that had a long, narrow front garden and wooden gate. On the opposite side of the path facing the gate, ran a stream or ditch. As I related this to my sitter, a spinning car wheel came into view. Then I saw that it was attached to a car that was lying upside down. The car was impacted against a tall pole. I could not move my focus from the wheel which continued to spin and block out further images. I cut the "reading" at that point – it had taken only a few minutes.

It was gratifying to have immediate confirmation of the details of the house, path and ditch, also the description of my sitter's Mother to whom the earring belonged and who was central to the reading. It was an extremely emotional experience for both of us, as I had not known that her Mother had died and my heart went out to her.

Afterwards I was horrified to learn that her Father had deliberately rammed their car into a telegraph pole during an argument and although he had tried to kill them all three, he and his young daughter had survived. He had only recently come out of prison after serving a sentence for manslaughter and his daughter, now eighteen, was desperately unhappy to be sharing a house with him. She came into the office the next day with a photograph of her Mother in the same silk dress with the cross-over bodice, standing in front of the gate of the brick house exactly as I had seen her.

One could question whether the message was complete and whether it had been facilitated by psychometry or telepathy as my sitter was naturally emotional and anxious to know if her Mother could possibly have survived. I have no doubt that her emotional state helped to achieve the positive results. I also know from the love that flowed over and through me, that it was a true spirit communication. Since then I have not questioned the source of my inspiration but have been content to convey evidential proof of survival whenever I could.

The happy consequence of the sitting was that George and Mary, John's parents, took her into their home. Unfortunately, and quite unforeseen, this triggered threats and harassment by her Father until police protection became necessary. Throughout this episode the love and support she received from her new friends was unconditional. We all believed she had been guided to my office at a time when she was in a potentially dangerous situation and in need of friends, spiritual upliftment and reassurance. Naturally she had been impressed by my reading and wanted to understand what had happened to her Mother. To this end we invited her to become part of our meditation and discussion group. This gave her the opportunity of learning about continuation of life beyond death and she came to understand that although human personality and intelligence survive death, any injury, disfigurement, pain or illness cease to exist with the death of the physical body. Where love has been strong the bonds of love cannot be broken – not even by death. Where our dear ones wish to help us along our way, they may at times be closer to us after their transition than they were before. But the choice is theirs – we cannot call them back. It is not desirable or right for us to cling to someone who has passed through the gateway to the other side of life, or mourn them to the extent that they are distressed for us and held back and prevented from progressing along their natural pathway.

When I gave sittings I found it practical and satisfying to insist that sitters did not volunteer information but respond with either "Yes" or "No". To allow the sitter to give information not only disrupts concentration but might influence the interpretation of what is being channelled. More importantly, it would not be evidential to sitters if they were allowed to volunteer information. In fact the best evidence is to be able to supply facts that are unknown to the sitter and require to be checked through a relative or by some other means.

A good, well developed medium does not need information from the sitter and should be able to rely entirely on her spirit guides. And as any message is only as good as the medium's accurate interpretation, it is important the medium *mentally* queries with the guide anything that is unclear before passing it on to the sitter. The aim of any sitting should be to provide evidential proof of survival and it follows that asking the sitter questions, or giving vague descriptions and generalisations do not achieve this goal.

1APTER 5 – THE POWER OF HEALING

Some time after the commencement of the Development Circle, Ron and I decided the time had come when we could no longer put off having our house decorated and set about making the necessary arrangements. It was a big effort to move furniture so that a decorator could work undisturbed in the bedrooms. But unfortunately it proved to be a disaster when the damp ceiling paper fell down and draped itself over the wardrobes and we had to take emergency measures. Which was how we came to be sleeping on a mattress on the sitting room floor!

When I awoke the following morning, I was absolutely stiff and could not turn or lift myself. Actually, this was not unusual as it had been a frequent recurring problem since our daughter had been born some eighteen years earlier. In a bed I could hold onto the edge of the frame as leverage and pull myself up, but here at floor level there was nothing to cling onto and I was helpless. Ron of course, was used to being asked to help and when I told him I could not move he did not reply but slid his arm round my waist and we lay quietly without a word. After a short time he said he would go and make a cup of tea and went into the nearby kitchen. I was still lying on my side facing the fireplace when I had the sudden sensation of a bucket of water being thrown at me at waist level and cascading down my lower body and legs. The water hit me hard and the strong pulsations continued for perhaps a minute and shocked, I shot upright with no effort at all! As I called out, Ron hurried in from the kitchen and I incredulously told him what had occurred.

I looked at him and asked "Did you try to heal me?" Self-consciously he smiled and admitted that he had tried and prayed and asked for proof that he could be a healer. It was then, intuitively recognising that I had experienced a wonderful powerful energy that I was inspired to say "Well, you have had your proof. You *can* heal, but you will never find it so easy again."

40

It was a peculiar off-the-cuff remark but I intuitively knew there was much hard work to do and a long way to go. And blessedly, after more than fifty years, I can confirm that I have never once had a repetition of that debilitating condition or anything like it.

It was the second miracle in my life as the first occurred when I was only 9 weeks old and had developed a grossly swollen foot. My parents took me to various hospitals who declined to admit me, but at a Paddington hospital it was found that I was suffering from a tropical disease inherited from my father who had been in the Egyptian Camel Corps during WW1, and it was assumed had drunk tainted water. This was quite likely as the Turks poisoned wells by throwing down bodies of men or camels to poison the water as they retreated. I was however, extremely ill and my parents were told I would not last the night. I still carry the scars of three slashes on the sole of my foot that were cut to release the poison and I was sent home with open wounds to ensure they drained cleanly. And there is no doubt that I made, what my parents called, a miraculous recovery.

Ron's healing of my long standing back condition whilst wonderfully beneficial to me, was I am sure, intended to prove to him that he could be a channel for healing. And a little later when a healing clinic was formed under the guidance of an experienced healer and we set about getting our qualifications from the Guild of Spiritualist Healers, he and I happily formed one of the teams. It was then that the power and truth of Spiritual healing began to manifest itself and the clinic's four teams were able to bring about wonderful relief and cures. Most were routine and have paled into insignificance over the years, although they were nonetheless effective at the time and on clinic evenings there was always a queue of people waiting for attention. Others stand out vividly in my memory.

I well recall one young man in his teens who came to the clinic and joined those who not only filled the reception room but overflowed onto the stairs. It was some considerable time before his turn came, and he limped into our room saying he had injured his leg and was in a lot of pain. We asked him to sit on a chair and Ron administered to his spine whilst I sat on a stool in front of him, first holding his hands and then paying attention to his leg. The patient was then asked to stand up and Ron worked on his leg

41

whilst he was standing. Afterwards I asked the young man to walk to the far corner of the room. He strode there!

When I smiled and said "There. How is that then?" He tersely replied "Well, that's what I came for, isn't it?" Hardly gracious, but he had indeed got what he came for. The following week a patient marvelled that she had seen him running to the bus station after his healing session.

Such cases of faith are in contrast to those patients, of which there were far too many, who turned up at the clinic every week, and when asked how they were, responded, "Well, I have had a good week, until this morning when it (sic) started aching again." Psychologically they were ready for their weekly dose of 'aspirin'. One may be forgiven for thinking that with a little more belief and faith they might have overcome the weekly cycle. But we would not refuse help to anyone who asked for it, neither would we accept personal payment although it was often offered. A church collection box was on display in the reception, but our services were free to all who came.

Hannah, a lady in her 60's who lived in the nearby market town of Alcester was recommended to the clinic and brought to us by her son. She was heavily built and severely arthritic, and it took much leverage and several pairs of kind hands to get her up the stairs and into our room. It was obvious she was experiencing a great deal of pain and a blessing that she obtained some relief on her first visit. Encouraged by the improvement she came to us regularly and eventually after many weeks, she was able to discard one of her walking canes. It took several months before she could walk freely and after many years of suffering was able to resume a normal life, walking to the nearby shops and doing her own housework. I have no doubt that her own belief in spiritual help made a large contribution to our outstanding success.

At this time Ron and I had two helpers who sat in the room with us. One was John's mother Mary, an experienced healer herself, and the other Viv whose diamond ring I had found earlier. Viv was a treasure to the Healing Group and she was one of the nicest, kindest and most spiritual people one could wish to meet. Her manner towards everyone she met radiated love and goodness. The power from these two helpers contributed in no small amount to our success but the main source of healing energy emanated from the spirit doctors who worked through Ron. The force was tangible. Everyone in the room could all feel the heat that flowed through him and there were times when healers and patient would be bathed in perspiration.

There were two remarkable occasions when healers and patient saw healing energy radiating like porcupine quills from his palms. He was working with his hands about ten centimetres from Hannah's ankle and the "quills" bridged the gap. The thin shafts of light were clear, brilliant lilac - a sight never forgotten by those present, except of course Ron who was unaware of the phenomena. Both occasions reinforced our belief that we were instruments of a benign and natural force, although not pretending to understand the energies involved.

During healing Ron would be overshadowed by his guide, an elderly doctor. Not only would his facial features alter and his voice change, but his posture would become that of a bent old man. The change was so dramatic that even those who were not psychic were able to identify the guide's presence before he had spoken. This dear mentor made himself known to us from the earliest days of the clinic and remained with us through all our activities. He would be with us the instant we wished to start healing, usually before the patient was seated – never once was there delay or reason for disappointment. His love and guidance were palpable and we have always had the greatest respect for him and felt secure in his hands. It is known that "like" on the earth plane attracts "like" from the spirit world and his guide was so similar to Ron that it was uncanny. When in the early days I made the mistake of asking his name, I was politely brushed aside. I have never forgotten his reply which was, "Who I am does not matter. It is the work that counts."

It was evident he delighted in working through Ron who was also modest and unassuming. I believe that it was this lack of ego, this humility, that helped to provide an open channel through which the healing energies could freely flow.

A special and personal instance of healing was when Ron's brother Vernon paid a visit to our home. It was a rare event as they were not a close family, Ron's two elder brothers having left home in their teens. Consequently, neither he nor his wife Eileen knew anything of our interest in the esoteric. Vernon was certainly not religious in the traditional sense, but neither was he agnostic or irreligious either. During the afternoon, somehow, and one never knows how these things start, conversation veered away from the norm and we were telling them of the healing clinic. A highly qualified engineer used to thinking in terms of black and white, Vernon thought it too nebulous and high flown for his taste. We couldn't have expected him to be other than sceptical and derisive and it was evident he thought his youngest brother had taken leave of his senses, or was under the power of some machinations of mine! Ron, meanwhile, was silently asking his guide to get him "out of this mess" and if it were possible, to provide his brother with some proof.

Suddenly Vernon exclaimed, "What's going on here? What are you doing to me?" He wrenched off his shoes and stood up. As he hobbled across the carpet we could see that without his specially made shoes he could only walk on the outside of his feet. He told us that the last items of clothing he took off at night before getting into bed were his shoes as he could not bear the pain of standing up without them. This was news to us. However, he accepted that magically he had been able to walk across our room without shoes and without pain, and generously acknowledged that something peculiar had happened. He then asked us to give him healing, the effect of which was very good and sustained for several months. It would have been remarkable if one session had been enough, and we would have liked to have seen him regularly. But it was not to be as he lived in the south of England, several hours journey away.

That visit and the healing, forged a new relationship between the two brothers and for several years we joined up to go abroad for our holidays. It was then that Vernon welcomed a hands-on healing session before we went out each evening, with excellent results. Vernon was quite intrigued with the whole process and he took the opportunity when he and Ron were alone, to enquire further into our beliefs, and I believe Ron was able to talk to him in some depth.

In earlier years before we had started holidaying together, Vernon had suffered a cancerous growth in his neck and had blessedly recovered after radiation treatment. But later, when in his seventies, he had a severe heart attack and had to be resuscitated, he knew his quality of life would never be the same. He hated the thought of living life as an invalid and privately told his son-in-law Bob, that he had no wish to recover on those terms. Within a couple of days he died quietly and contentedly. How much his courage can be attributed to Ron's influence may only be surmised, but undoubtedly, his attitude towards life and death had undergone a profound change after he had experienced our healing.

In the clinic we worked as separate teams and patients would invariably see the same healer each time. However, sometimes a quality would be lacking, perhaps an incompatibility at some level, and the healing would not be effective. Another team would then be asked to take the patient over and this often had better results. But there are no guarantees in healing, all is carried out by the Grace of God, and as a healer, all one asks is that patients approach the healing session with an open mind, and do not put up an invisible but tangible barrier of scepticism.

Although not connected with the clinic there was the memorable occasion when Ron and I were on holiday in Looe. We had rented a cottage on the sea front with two friends, both healers in a church some distance from our own. The holiday had passed happily, Ron drawing while I painted and our friends explored the area. Two weeks passed very quickly and the final Saturday morning had arrived with the two cars packed, ready at the door for the journeys home. Everything was clean and tidy but I did a last minute fussing around during which I tried to straighten an armchair. Not realising it was a heavy, iron framed bed-settee I had raised it only two or three inches before it slipped through my fingers onto the big toe of my foot. The nail split from top to bottom. We were all aghast but I quickly asked for a bowl of hot water and rejecting all suggestion of getting a doctor, asked one of the men to dash to the main street and get bandages. By the time it had been bathed half the nail was standing up like a sail and it took firm bandaging to press it down. All this time the toe felt burning hot and it was agreed I had been badly shaken and should go and lie down.

I went into the first bedroom I came to. It was not one we had used and finding a double bunk for children, I rolled onto the bottom bed. As I lay on my side I was feeling very sorry for myself and at the same time guilty for putting everyone to so much trouble. Suddenly I became aware of an old man with white hair and exceptionally rosy cheeks sitting in the far corner diagonal to the bed. The light around him was very bright. He smiled and held out his arms which stretched right across the room until his hands cupped around my foot without actually touching it. As he radiated power and love I felt a wave of contentment and said "Thank you. God bless you," and promptly fell fast asleep! I have no doubt that at about the same time Ron and the other two healers would have been sending me love and healing prayers too.

When I awoke some three hours later it was to find that the owners of the cottage had phoned to say that they would not be using the property that weekend and we could stay an extra two days. The cars had already been off loaded! That afternoon I walked with the others a short distance to local gardens and climbed steep steps to a seat overlooking the beach and the sea. Incredibly I experienced no pain, neither that afternoon nor any at time in the future, although the nail was bandaged or plastered until it became whole some seven or eight months later.

That dear Healing Guide has helped at other times when I have been able to bring relief to others who have injured hands or feet. Personally, I think I am more careless than most as I have since injured my toes and fingers on several occasions. Particularly nasty was when I was helping to build a rockery in our garden, and dropped a boulder on the same big toe! At the first opportunity I have quietly pictured this dear old man with his rosy cheeks, sat in a brightly lit part of a room and asked for his help. He has never let me down, and although shaken, I have never experienced pain from my injuries which have taken the normal time, and yards of plaster, to heal.

Healing is a natural power and energy that is freely available. If someone in discomfort or pain believes in the benevolence and power of the spirit world and asks for healing for himself, it is possible that he may find he can draw to himself the Divine healing energy. This is not to be confused with positive thought which can be applied to cheering ourselves up or looking at the compensations in life. It is everything to do with recognising that healing is a natural energy emanating from God the source of all energies. To pray to God (or the Super Intelligence as I liked to think of It at that time) and ask for help, creates the right conditions for healing to manifest.

Spiritual healers work as the instruments of doctors in the spirit world who desire to continue to help mankind from the other side of the veil. They have learned to channel the healing energy through the mediumship of Spiritual Healers to their patients. The energy is directed to a spiritual aspect of the patient (the aura) which in turn reacts on the physical body via the energy centres known as the chakras. It is therefore essential that patient and healer are in harmony with each other and channels are open to allow this unique energy to flow. As with the medical profession, it isn't possible to always obtain a cure, but with this type of healing, where there is no obstruction, it is always possible to obtain a measure of relief and betterment - without the use of drugs. And whilst mentioning drugs, a Spiritual Healer should never under any circumstances advise the withdrawal of drugs or medicines that have been prescribed by a medical practitioner. But he may of course, advise the patient to speak to his doctor to see if certain medicines or drugs are still necessary for his wellbeing.

Spiritual healing is the blend of a natural energy and the compassion of a healer who doesn't heal, but is merely a channel for the manifestation to take place. The ability to do so is one of the Gifts of the Spirit, but it is desirable for healers to undertake training and work within a code of conduct that conforms to the codes of practices laid down by the medical profession, dentists, midwives and veterinary surgeons. This protects both healer and patient from malpractice. In this context, the approach to Spiritual healing is that it should always be regarded as a complementary therapy and not an alternative to orthodox medicine.

CHAPTER 6 – JOURNEY WITH A MONK

Our church premises proved to be a convenient central venue and services were always well attended, but to widen our appeal and bring our ideals to more people, I organised publicity meetings. The committee agreed that although we would have to pay heavier expenses for first class national and international mediums, it would be well worth while. I was aware that inviting the Press had its risks as it could potentially expose us to ridicule from a profession usually seeking to promote the sensational side of our "ism". However, because of the high standard of these very special mediums who could be relied upon to give evidence of survival, I decided to invite Donald, chief reporter on the local paper, The Redditch Indicator, and got to know him well, not only through these meetings, but also in the general way of business and was pleased that he gave us very fair write-ups, sometimes even enthusiastic. He was a tall, lean, untidy figure with a straggly beard and bright humorous eyes. An interesting man who had previously enquired into various forms of Extra Sensory Perception (E.S.P). and was adept at self-hypnosis, although he was ignorant of our philosophy.

When, one afternoon, the receptionist 'phoned through to say that Donald was asking to see me, I said he should be shown to an interview room and found him seated on a settee with a young reporter next to him, notebook at the ready.

Apologetically Donald started, "I'm sorry to barge in like this in working hours, but we have a something that's turned up in a field, and I'm wondering if you can identify it for me? It's rather important."

"Well", I replied taken aback. "I'll look at it. But it's not convenient to do anything with it at the moment. And," glancing towards the young reporter, "I wouldn't wish my name to be published in association with anything psychic." My natural wish to protect my business interests was readily understood. Fishing in his pocket, Donald agreed. "Of course. I understand that. But please look at it. I can leave it with you, but it is rather urgent."

As he spoke he handed me a small piece of metal about three quarters of an inch high and the same in width. It was fashioned like a small crown and if I had been asked to guess what it was, I might have said, "A knob from an ancient pot or vase." It was difficult to say what the metal was, but it appeared to be lead which, over time, had become coated with a white substance. He went on, "Whatever the outcome, I can promise you that you will not be named or identified. I would just be grateful if you would do it." With that reassurance and believing he could be trusted, I told him I would take it home and contact him in a day or two.

Even as I spoke I became aware of a figure of a monk who came through the closed door and was now standing in front of me, and followed on by saying, "But there is a monk in a long brown habit who has just come into the room!"

There was no choice but to go on, so I asked them to sit quietly and please, not to volunteer any information. Closing my eyes I began a clairvoyant journey that I recited as it occurred. I have the clearest recollection of following the monk into country surroundings and along the outside wall of a grey stone building. We turned left and rounded a corner and proceeded down the side of a longer wall until we came to a short flight of four or five stone steps that led down into a long rectangular room. The dimness was relieved by light from burning rushes that were held in iron conical shaped containers fixed at intervals along the wall. A scrubbed refractory table ran three quarters of the way down the centre of the room and it had benches on either side. The table was set with wooden bowls.

The monk led me to the far end of the room where a small altar table stood central against the wall. The wall itself was completely covered by an intricate ornamental screen that was beautifully crafted in a trellis design with leaves, tendrils and roses. The monk walked across to the right hand side of the screen and smilingly pointed to a rose the centre of which was missing. He had the "crown" in his hand and holding it on its side placed it exactly into the space at the heart of the rose. Still smiling at me he turned to leave and indicated by extending his hand that I should follow him outside. As I reached the top of the steps the familiar outline of the Malvern Hills met my view and I knew we were facing west. I was also shown orchards heavy with rosy apples and dotted with beehives and knew the monks produced mead and cider for their livelihood.

I also saw an armoured man on horseback carrying a lance who charged out of the orchard, knocking down a monk who was working there. The armoured man came with several others, but they disappeared from my sight.

The vision faded and I was back with the journalists. It had been so crystal clear that I immediately volunteered to sketch a plan of the building which I described as having upper rounded windows and appeared to be colonnaded among other things. Donald was on the point of telling me about the field where the metal had been found but I stopped him as I felt other artefacts might follow, as indeed they later did.

It was a couple of weeks later when an entire page of the local newspaper was devoted to an account of finding a buried chapel at Bentley in the Worcestershire countryside. Donald had taken a water diviner from a local utility company to the site to see what he might find, but had not told him about my plan. The newspaper article related that by using his skill as a dowser, the man, Mr Greenaway, had found and traced the buried foundations of a building. The plan he drew exactly co-ordinated with my own. By placing our two drawings together where I showed downward steps he had found a gap. In all other respects our drawings were identical. The dimensional proportions and the building's relation to the western hills were confirmed. An expert from the Department of Archaeology at Birmingham University had previously visited the site and judged the building to be mediaeval (13th/14th century) from the many small pieces of pottery the local farmer was constantly unearthing, but he had been unable to identify the small "crown" of lead. Hence my involvement!

Apparently there are existing records of a small chapel in Bentley that was associated with Bordesley Abbey in Redditch, but not much in the way of history or detail, but neither Mr Greenaway or myself were aware of this. The article in the newspaper emphasised the remarkable detailed "journey" I had taken and was highly complimentary about my mediumistic skills.

And Donald had kept his word and not identified me although he mentioned the Spiritualist Church which obviously did them no harm.

Some time later there was an archaeological dig on the site when more pieces of the screen were unearthed exactly where I had shown on my plan. Later there were some small pieces of bone in an adjacent field that I identified as being part of a magnificent chestnut horse. When I described the cottage near his stable and an adjacent oak, I was told these still existed. But I declined to go to the site being satisfied that I had played my part in helping Donald with his enquiries and at the same time had done something to recompense him for his objective reporting of our meetings. And he gave me the lead "crown" as a keepsake of this unusual event, which of course, I still have together with the newspaper article.

This incident was important to me as it expanded my understanding of a fourth dimension of time. It placed us in the middle of a road from where it is possible to travel not only forward but also backward. Not just recent events could be seen, but events in the past were evidently still clear. That it is demonstrably possible to see both the future and the past, suggests certain events that affect not only individuals but the world in general, already exist in another dimension. Shakespeare may have had something like this in mind when he wrote that all the world is a stage and men and women merely players. But actors are tied to a script, whilst in the real world, we have choice and freewill within the parameters allowed us, and are responsible for our own actions.

CHAPTER 7 – A MEASURE OF UNDERSTANDING

In spite of my small success with psychometric readings, I felt no temptation to give demonstrations on church platforms. By nature I aspire to perfection, and did not consider myself competent for such work. I certainly did not want to join the ranks of underdeveloped mediums who give vague messages full of generalisations to pad out the time allotted to them. Whilst to some extent entertaining, and sometimes amusing, the ego of such mediums may be more easily satisfied than the congregation. Being strong on organisation it suited me to organise meetings and social events, produce a regular church magazine and run a bookstall. We had an enthusiastic team and raised funds by jumble sales, garden parties, suppers and outings. It all helped towards building a successful and living church.

At the same time I was running my own successful business and chairing other professional organisations – there were not enough hours in a day. They were blessed times when I was at peak physical energy and privileged to feel very close to those in the spirit world who were guiding me. Although at that time I was unaware of the strong influence the Ego has on our thinking, I had an inkling of the need for balance between the material and the spiritual in our daily lives, but there were so many demands on my time that it seemed an impossibility to change my life in any way.

The need for balance had been prompted to a large extent by reading of the need for what was called "right thinking". The author Hamblin propounded a positive belief in the existence of a Divine order and a Divine pattern in all things. He encouraged readers to believe that the Divine Love of God is manifest in all things, and that even when events seem to be conspiring against us, the hand of God is guiding us towards an unseen and unknown betterment.

Initially it was difficult to believe that we are always in the right place at the right time as my domestic situation was difficult due to continual interference from my mother-in-law and Ron's guilt at what he saw as his part in her unhappiness. But through study I found I could accept this difficult situation as being part of my spiritual development, knowing it to be transient and believing that what really matters is not the problem but how we deal with it.

It was also around this time that I studied the work of Ian Stevenson who most carefully and meticulously investigated re-incarnation and proved beyond doubt that some children were able to recall previous lives – memories that faded when they were about 6 years old. His work was carried on by Jim B. Tucker who wrote 'Return to Life' about extraordinary cases of children who remember past lives. He also found adults who were disfigured and marked by injuries sustained at the death of their previous life. It was difficult not to conclude that at least some people are able to reincarnate, but that posed the question – why only some or do we all follow the same path?

These and other questions were opening doors for me and my perception of myself as a spiritual being living a human life, took a huge leap forward. Nothing can stop our spiritual growth and unfoldment, although we progress at our own pace and in our own time according to our spiritual awareness and our desire to do so. It is part of the natural order that each soul will develop, expand and grow although it may take interminable time to make considerable progress. But spiritual growth is inevitable and it is in the nature of man to do so.

Thus it was that I began to appreciate the need for conscious thought control and came to understand not only that we are what we have thought, but we will become what we now think. Our thoughts, singularly and collectively, are the breeding ground for so much suffering and disharmony that we often erroneously attribute to God. We ask why certain events are allowed to happen, overlooking the fact that they have been set in motion by mans own thoughts and subsequent actions. Thoughts are a powerful energy and the motivation for all we do. Unconstrained thoughts of criticism, envy or other negatives, will create disharmony and division, and certainly generate unhappiness and ill-health in ourselves. Conversely, thinking positively, compassionately and charitably draws people to us and we become the recipients of kindness, friendship and love.

From childhood I had been taught that God was the ultimate arbiter and that everyone would be judged responsible for his own actions. I believed, and still do, that revenge is not mine to give. But my thoughts on personal responsibility had strengthened since I had found its inclusion in the principles of the Spiritualist Church, together with the parallel concept that after our passing there would be compensation and retribution for our actions here on earth. It is up to each living person to strive to live to his highest moral understanding and to cling to principles of absolute Love, order, wholeness, harmony and infinite Goodness.

I came upon the statement that "Of ourselves we can do nothing, and without God we *are* nothing. We *are*, because God *is.*" But I was not ready to take this on board or understand it. Being successful in all aspects of my material life through hard work, diligence and a will to succeed, albeit sometimes aggressively, I was naturally proud of *my* achievements and had confidence in *myself* and *my* own abilities. The statement that "without God we are nothing" seemed to undermine and diminish me as a person and it was only much later that I came to understand who we truly are, and the power of the Ego in our lives.

CHAPTER 8 – SPIRIT COMMUNICATION

Although we differed in our rate of development, the church circle members gradually came to identify their own Gifts of the Spirit and recognised that the bond that united us was the gift of healing. It was as though we had been brought together for that specific purpose.

We found we were open to communication with the spirit world through inspiration, intuition, clairvoyance, and later, as we progressed, through healing. Those in the world of spirit may desire to get in touch with us and can do so if they are able, but their contact with us is always voluntary and we are unable to impinge on their world as they can on ours. We cannot call back the so-called dead. But if we are sensitive and have the *right motives*, we can facilitate contact with guides and guardian angels. Under their guidance and protection we can attune ourselves to become a medium or channel through which communication and healing energies may flow.

It has been pointed out earlier that it is not difficult for spirit entities to contact sitters especially when the latter are endeavouring to make contact purely for amusement. Toying with ouija boards, or other meaningless practises, has no place in Spiritualism as they can be an attraction to mischievous or inferior spirits who are still attached to the earth plane. Spirits who were anti-social or mischievous in their lifetime may seek to influence those still here, or take delight in playing tricks on those unaware of the dangers. Such communication might seem fun at the time but the results could be deeply disturbing and harmful, and what is more, difficult to dispel. To sit alone or with others, for the sole purpose of trying to contact the spirit realms is a reckless exercise.

There are others who have taken a normal transition but do not recognise their state of survival. They may have led decent, ordinary lives but because of their ignorance remain nearer to the earth's physical vibrations than those of the next plane. Unfortunately, some who remain close to the earth stay attached to their old familiar surroundings and whilst not meaning any harm, may disturb those sensitive to their presence, as was the case in my father-in-law's house. People do not become saints when they pass into the next life, neither do they suddenly acquire wisdom and light. They are *exactly* the same as when they were here. They pass into the next world with the same intelligence and the same spiritual understanding, the same prejudices and the same principles. As has been said, and it bears repeating, to sit without the protection of an experienced medium and her known guides and guardian angels, is similar to opening the doors of one's home and inviting any stranger to enter.

There are no short cuts to the valuable years of training that are essential to establish knowledge of one's guides and helpers and develop clear intercommunication. A humbleness of heart is essential. Those who embark on this path purely to satisfy their ego may achieve success as clairvoyants or psychics but rarely achieve deep understanding of spiritual values. Indeed, they will often go through their lives absolving their own weaknesses and shortcomings as just "being human", not realising the extent of spiritual growth that can be achieved in an earthly lifetime.

When establishing communication with the spirit world, it is our responsibility to provide conditions of sincere prayer, love and harmony. These are essential characteristics of a successful development circle, healing group or church. If negative qualities such as envy, back-biting, resentment, discontent, grandiosity or egotism are allowed to intrude, groups will never attain the harmony and tranquillity that our guides and guardian angels require to do their best work. Further, if negative qualities exist, we may be opening ourselves to undesirable communication with those in the lower realms of the spirit world and their harmful influence.

By deep, sincere prayer in which we let it be known that we wish to contact only the highest sources of inspiration and wisdom, we can create the right conditions for uniting with the highest spiritual beings it is possible for us to contact. In a group where harmony prevails, our vibrations and sensitivity are heightened and we are able to join with those on the next plane who are reaching out to us and who have made it their mission to guard and guide us. It is in this context that the principle of "like" attracting "like" manifests itself and we find that those with whom we are in communication are those most compatible with our innermost selves. And after many years of sittings and meetings our group had not the slightest doubt that we were guarded and guided by highly evolved and loving Beings of Light.

Notwithstanding this confidence, we were mindful of our earliest instruction that spirit communication must always be under our control. Meetings always opened and closed in prayer and guides were blessed for their presence and guidance. At other times, when alone and going about our daily business, we received inspiration and flashes of intuition which were recognised as guidance, but which at all times, were subject to our own free will. Control is always essential and spirits should never be allowed to infringe upon us without our permission. It must be understood that they can easily be told to go away at any time that is inconvenient.

The church was thriving. It was a centre where harmony and friendship blossomed. As is so often the case in the pioneering days of an organisation, there were many enthusiastic helpers keen to increase the congregation and expand church activities. However, along the way we naturally had setbacks and difficulties, some of which, at the time, were worrying. Not the least was John's career move to London, and the fact that the building in which we held public services and the healing clinic, was to be demolished to make way for redevelopment. At first it seemed that we might not be able to find other suitable premises, and there was natural concern for the future. But we did not recognise the guidance we were receiving! The hall we eventually obtained was much better and large enough to seat about two hundred people. More than ample for weekly services and adequate enough to hold publicity meetings. Unfortunately, being a public hall, we could not adapt it to provide individual privacy at the healing clinic - something we considered to be the ideal. It then occurred to me that by moving the clinic into my offices and allowing the four healing teams to each use a room on Monday evenings, the final part of our problem could be solved. It was gratifying that the healing teams found the new conditions congenial, and easy to work in. When we had settled, we were able to recognise that good, even betterment, had come out of a seemingly hopeless situation. It is part of the human condition for problems and troubles to come into our lives that, at the time, can seem so devastating that we feel overwhelmed. But where we with our limited vision can see only the problem, elsewhere threads are being drawn together and benefits are waiting to come into existence. We can only try to have faith and accept that all experiences are for our ultimate good and that patience and trust should be our watch-word. It is no bad thing to always regard one's cup as being half full and never half empty!

The healing that took place in the new clinic was excellent. From the outset Ron had been adamant that he would not affect to have medical skills. Consequently he had rejected the idea that he and I should wear white coats, and the other three teams followed our example. He was more than willing to allow himself to be a channel through which spirit doctors could work, and he succeeded in disassociating himself from preconceived ideas about a patient's condition. By setting aside his own personality and allowing his old guide and friend to over-shadow him, he was able to work entirely by prayer and faith. He functioned in a trance or semi-trance state, mostly unaware of his surroundings and what was actually taking place. In this way he provided an open channel of the purest kind without any pretension that it was in any way due to his own skills.

It was commonplace for a patient to come into our room complaining of a particular pain or discomfort, but for Ron's hands to be directed to another part of the body where the seat of the condition lay, or a more pressing problem needed attention. An instance was when a man came with a sprained ankle but Ron's hands were taken to heal his stomach! It was only afterwards when both conditions had been attended to, that it was revealed that the patient had vomited earlier in the day.

It comes naturally to me to "mirror" patients' conditions, reflecting their aches and pains onto my own physical body, which helps to identify where healing is required and ensures that the energy is being directed positively. Clairvoyance too, has often proved to be a vital part of healing sessions. Often the outward manifestation is only a reflection of an underlying problem. It is not unusual to visualise something in the past or present that may be the root cause of the patient's current condition. There were times when we became aware of a relative or friend of the patient who although now in the world of spirit had come to watch the healing. This was a tremendous news for the patients and played a valuable part in the healing process.

An illustration of this combination of healing and clairvoyance occurred when we were visiting a patient in her home and she asked if we would have time to see another lady. She told us that Sue, who was cleaning in the house, was suffering from headaches and stomach pains and needed help. Of course we readily agreed and a slim, pale young woman in her thirties was called into the room. Ron became aware of her chaotic state of mind as she came in – even before she was seated. After introductions and when she was settled, we asked her to take three or four deep breaths and then whilst listening to her own breathing, try to relax. "Mirroring" her symptoms I felt dizzy with the confusion racing through her head. However, she responded well to the calming affect of the healing and within a short time had fallen asleep. Sitting in front and holding her hands, I "saw" a young girl who impressed me as being her daughter and the source of the distress and confusion. The young girl was pregnant and her mother, our patient, had been plunged into despair and turmoil. In normal circumstances she would have kept her problems to herself but when later I counselled her, she was only too pleased to unburden herself and confirm what I had seen. She told us that her family was living in a small house on a tight budget and she did not know how they were going to manage. She was trying to cope with three part-time jobs and was neither eating nor sleeping well. No wonder she was at her wits end and showing all the signs of debilitating stress.

At the same time as I was identifying her underlying problem, Ron had been guided to assuage her agitation by directing the healing energy to her head, stomach and central nervous system. It was whilst he was working that he became aware of our patient's mother standing to one side, fascinated by what was going on. Through Ron she conveyed her love and wished Sue to know that she was always with her, although up till now they hadn't been able to communicate. This message, with a detailed description of her mother, was accepted with astonishment. It was something completely new! Something Sue had never dreamed or imagined and an unexpected bonus to the healing.

We were able to see her several times when we visited the house, and by the Grace of God were able to help her through this stressful time by further healing and *inspirational* counselling. Her mother's presence had made a tremendous impression and for the first time Sue had become aware of the possibility of an afterlife, and realised that there is more to life here than is outwardly seen. Although it was difficult, she became resigned to her problems in a much calmer way, without resentment, realising that they *would* pass and that life is but one phase after another. Sadly there was very little that could be done to improve matters materially and she accepted that the best she could do was to support her daughter in whatever way open to her, then leave her problems to God and the guardian angels who had them both in their loving care. I was able to give her literature to help her to understand this new way of looking at life and from our point of view, healing apart, we were happy to have opened a door for her.

A blend of healing, clairvoyance and counselling under the guidance and inspiration of doctors and healers so much more advanced than ourselves, can bring unimaginable relief to those who ask for help. But healers and mediums need to be conscious that they are exerting considerable influence on others through the advice and counselling they give. They should know in their hearts that they are working from the highest motives and ensure that what they convey comes not from themselves, but emanates from the higher realms where knowledge and wisdom is far superior to their own.

It is true to say that not everyone benefits from spiritual healing as there are persons who are reluctant to be helped in this manner. They may have been persuaded against their will to attend a healing clinic, but because of an innate prejudice or fear, they unknowingly create an impenetrable barrier. We have known this to appear as a sheet of grey steel between us and the patient, and no amount of love or sympathy on our part could penetrate or dispel it. It is possible that such a patient may return at some other time in a different frame of mind, and accept the healing which is freely offered. We cannot help where there is resistance, although it may still possible to bring about a betterment by sending out healing in our prayers. In many instances absent healing is most effective and there are some wonderful results, but unfortunately, healers do not always hear of the outcome.

I think that today we now recognise that people's problems are often helped by talking to a counsellor at one of the multitude of counselling organisations that now exist. Back in the 1970's this was not the case and people often didn't know where to turn for help. But in the case I am about to relate the man's choice of counsellor was most appropriate.

For me it started when I was told a man had arrived in my office reception and asked to see me urgently. I recognised his name as the M.D. of a company with premises on the outskirts of Birmingham and I naturally thought he wanted to discuss some business. However, when he had sat down, without any pre-amble he told me that he had been referred to me by Kings Heath Spiritualist Church as his 22 year old son had committed suicide at University! He was completely lost and desperate to know what to think and, he pleaded, could I help?

Even as he spoke, his son came and stood at his shoulder and I was able to console him with the fact that his son was "alive" and had come to say how very sorry he was. My description of the young man in his slim fitting, high necked grey pullover, his smile and shock of hair were easily recognised and accepted by his Father. Remarkably I was then taken on a visionary tour of the young man's room at home. The tennis rackets behind the door, the hockey stick, the books, the pennants on the wall and the articles on top of a chest of drawers, were too much for his father and he just crumpled into tears. I am convinced that it had all been carefully arranged by spirit forces, as it was accomplished so easily and quickly. I have no idea what later ensued, but I am sure it was healing of the highest order and doors had been opened for the bereaved Father.

CHAPTER 9 – THE HOME CIRCLE

The church development circle disbanded when John left for London, which was quite a blow although all the members continued to be healers in the clinic. Ron and I, keen to study further development, invited some of our church friends to join us in forming a group at home. These were people who were prepared to commit themselves to regular weekly attendance and most stayed several years – one, Joy, for the whole eighteen years the circle was in existence. The meetings were focused on development of our Gifts of the Spirit, closer unity with our friends in spirit, and furtherance of our understanding of spiritual philosophy. Harmony was the keyword. A harmony that bound guides and sitters together without discord or envy. We were all seeking the spiritual freedom to unfold our innermost consciousness, and readily appreciated that we were only on the threshold of wisdom and understanding.

The format was set from the beginning. Ron was the natural leader and I opened the meetings with a prayer and brief address. Later, when we had become more comfortable with each other, members of the circle were encouraged to say either a healing or closing prayer. It was helpful if after the opening and healing prayers, I took the sitters into a guided meditation. Asking them to first visualise a royal blue velvet curtain, I invited them to go through it and into a corridor off which were many doors. Some were closed others open, but initially we always went to the far end and emerge into a lush green meadow glowing with wild flowers. Strolling down a gentle slope in the warm summer air, sitters would be released to their own meditation. Some would continue to the bank of a clear, running stream. Others might wander into the countryside to marvel at the clarity of light, the bright colours and abundance of nature. Or they might choose to lie on the bank where the water babbled musically over the pebbles. Here they could find peace and contentment. Others might sit or lie quietly in a far away field, breathing in pure air and listening to the silence. Or, perhaps best of all, they might drift into a meaningful vision which they would later recite to us. When they were asked to return, they would be refreshed and renewed by their timeless experience, ready for the main meditation of the evening. The full meditation is at the end of this book.

It was never difficult to find a subject for meditation. I would be drawn to a book or the bible, and most times, would open a page at random and find an appropriate short reading. The reading and the meditation always seemed to be right for that evening, both for ourselves and our spirit communicators, but I never felt that the choice had been mine. This method of selecting our theme allowed us to become familiar with various aspects of spiritual expression, and it served us well for some twelve years.

After that time of sitting together, and as the circle of friends on both sides of the veil drew closer, we were able to advance our meditations by dwelling on abstract concepts. Even those who normally would have found it difficult to think in abstract terms, found that Truth, Forgiveness, Beauty, Justice or other such concept, could be successfully meditated upon. This was a big advancement and during our evenings together I often had a psychic vision of a large umbrella covering the whole of the circle through which shone a golden light from above. And so it proved to be. Not only were we guarded and guided, but gradually we became united in our awareness and consciousness and often all arrived at the same interpretation and understanding of the evening's theme. We felt very close and very privileged.

It often happened that during meditation, a person would intrude into the field of my psychic vision and I would realise that an entity from the spirit world had been brought for help. In the early days it was preferable to speak quietly and let the others in the circle know of the entity's presence in order to lead them into understanding how to deal with the situation. Later when someone needing help was brought directly to one of them, they were able to deal with the entity without reservation or fear. These souls were always included in our closing prayer. This easy, familiar contact with the spirit world was a normal part of our work, and visits from those who needed help were always well controlled by our guides.

We all agreed that irrespective of our individual progress during the course of the evening, the highlight was always the address, through Ron, by one of his guides. This always occurred after the circle had closed and we would be sitting with cups of tea reviewing the events of the evening. Usually a man of few quiet words, he would talk at length in the voices of his guides, often animated and at great speed. In a kindly, benevolent way the guides would add to our discussion and often introduced a quite different point of view. Invariably we were left with new thoughts and ideas to take us forward. Ron delivered all this in a trance state and whilst he was aware of what was being said as it passed through his head, later he was unable to recall the precise content. There were some evenings when it would be our privilege to be able to converse with the guide on some point or another. Tape recordings were made at the meetings, typed the same week and given to sitters, so that these precious teachings could be studied at leisure. The circle experienced guidance of high order and we had no doubt of the veracity and quality of what we were being taught.

Being eager to learn, we found it difficult when told by Ron's guide not to rush into matters beyond our comprehension as there was no point in infants trying to cope with sixth form stuff. But there was good reason for this advice. A pattern emerged in which we would be given a new concept or philosophical idea. It would then seem that during the following few weeks we would be marking time and not making progress. In reality, the new philosophy would be consolidating within and becoming part of our understanding, after which we would be ready to take another small step forward. In this way we absorbed our new knowledge not only with our intellect but also at a deeper consciousness and higher spiritual level. It was as though the flower of spiritual understanding was slowly opening within us.

In retrospect one can see that the purpose of our first meetings at John's house had been to lead us to know our Gifts of the Spirit and become aware of the closeness of those who have made it their work to guard and guide us. Almost from the outset I had become aware of an Arab in white robes with whom I could mentally communicate. His presence was made known to me by a peculiar itching, as though I had a moustache, after which I would see him standing or kneeling before me. After greeting me with the traditional salaam of his earthly race, he would wait for me to mentally respond after which he would impress upon me whatever he wished to convey. I have been aware that this dear soul has been my guide and mentor for over thirty years and probably, even before that. It has been many years since he stood back to allow Ephriam, an ancient philosopher, to come close to impress and inspire me. A dear man who now has a strong influence on me, such as when I am writing this book. But my dear Egyptian friend promised he would always be on hand when needed. And so it has proved to be. His steadfastness and love have been the bedrock of my faith and have carried me through many difficult periods.

It is useful to state here the limit of my understanding in the early days of our home circle. I asserted that we humans have a spirit that existed before we came on the earth and will continue to exist after we physically die. It was plain that for an ethereal spirit to exist and function in this physical environment, it requires to be clothed in a body made of the elements of the earth plane. The physical body is that outer garment and also the temple of the spirit within. It is natural and inevitable that the body will deteriorate and die and it is then that the spirit will be released into the next stage of its eternal existence. And this process may be repeated time and time again as the spirit evolves.

I was prompted by the simple analogy that can be seen in the incredible changes that a caterpillar has to undergo to become a beautiful butterfly or moth. As one outer covering dies another takes its place, but can we deny that it is the same life force or spirit which animates all stages of the metamorphosis?

There is no break in the continuity of life. Only change. A change of consciousness and a gentle sliding from one state to another. Those who have led a selfish life, grabbing all advantages for themselves, or lived an anti-social existence whether within or outside the home, will have imposed a deep stain on their spiritual character. But where the opposite is true and they have been helpful to others and tried to live by higher principles, their spiritual light will shine for all to see. Most of us are an amalgam of virtues and lighter stains; very few are so depraved as to be all bad; none on this plane are all good. It is the Law of Cause and Effect that determines where we will find ourselves after passing, and all will be led forward when they are ready to progress.

Our natural communication with the spirit world, and the evidence we received in church and circle, led us to firmly believe in the immortality of the human soul and the survival of individual personality. It is at this point that many rest content and seek no further illumination, thereby spending the rest of their earthly lives in a half awakened state. Those who venture to look deeper and seek to understand how our existence here fits into a wider plan, become blessed and stimulated into living their lives to greater purpose. To live in Truth, is to have belief in an afterlife and belief in an eternity wherein the human soul may progress to the Godhead from which it came. The cycle is a natural process in which we are all involved irrespective of our religious or cultural convictions or our material circumstances.

Our guides consistently told us that this world is a place of opportunity for spiritual growth and advancement. And whilst we enter this lifetime not knowing our purpose or the weaknesses we carry, we believe that we are born into the environment and circumstances that allow us opportunities for spiritual advancement. It is not easy to accept that adversity should be regarded as necessary for personal development. But it is certainly true that we learn more through hard times than on those sunny days when we are happy and all is going well.

Recognition of the need for the spiritual growth is a first step towards to progress, but however much effort we put into our desired advancement it will not be possible to achieve perfection in this lifetime. We should not feel dispirited if at times we take one step sideways or even two back. This is part of the human condition and we will be given many opportunities to refine those aspects of our spiritual nature that we recognise need to be improved. Some, overwhelmed and pre-occupied with the pressures of material matters, may reach an advanced age before they are attracted to a spiritual pathway. Some may never give it deep thought. But eventually all will set their feet on the path, either in this world or the next, and all will work their way through the planes of the unseen world. Time is unimportant and as we will later see, cannot be measured in our known terminology.

CHAPTER 10 – KNOW YOURSELF

An outing for church members to the Spiritualist Association of Great Britain in London, led to the discovery of excellent books on Spiritualist philosophy. They opened up new avenues of thought and new perspectives on a wide range of perplexities. One particular book that is still available is The Spirits Book by Allan Kardec. It is a collection of teachings by spirits of high degree transmitted through various mediums, and set in order by a man of remarkable insight and wisdom. The contents are laid out as questions and answers and range from the nature of man and the nature of the spirit world, to morality, ignorance, sin, repentance, God, plurality of existences, and the natural and spiritual Laws governing our existence. It was another breakthrough in attempting to understand the deeper truths behind our church services and our interaction with the spirit world.

As with all writings on this complex subject there will always be passages or concepts which at first reading, are beyond our comprehension or acceptance. But this should not cause concern as we are all at different stages of understanding. Doubtless at some future time, a reader will pick up the same writing that has perplexed him in the past and find no difficulty in absorbing aspects which previously were beyond him. This is common occurrence and can come as a revelation to the reader who may not have realised that he had progressed; progression being so slow and imperceptible!

However, reading philosophical books should not lead us into thinking that we know the Truth of all there is. The whole Truth is not accessible to us in this lifetime, and will never be. But such teachings may bring us a little nearer to understanding the righteousness of natural Laws and encourage us to re-examine our ideas and attitudes towards living. It is clear to me that our reason for being is to acquit ourselves in this life so that after the change we call death, we may evolve to a stage in the next life on the Astral Plane befitting our spiritual state and understanding. Whether we realise it or not, or whether we follow any particular religion or not, we are all embarked on a continual cycle of death and rebirth. There will be many lifetimes, either here or elsewhere, before we attain perfection, but in this lifetime we can aspire to goodness, virtue and moral improvement.

Some come into this lifetime with an innate goodness that is evident for all to see, and they shine like beacons in the darkness of the corporeal world. Others lack decency or moral values, either by reason of their own spiritual ignorance, or by having been corrupted by the environment into which they were born. But all come here to learn from their experiences. It is after we pass through the gateway of death that we will be able to review and judge our life here. Then we shall be able to see the justice of finding ourselves raised to the degree that we have made progression.

Our circle teachings were urging us "to elevate ourselves such that we are able to gain knowledge and understanding of true life." During meditation we found we were able to raise our vibrations to meet with those on the spirit plane who lower theirs to communicate with us. We were told of the desirability of carrying this higher state of consciousness into our daily lives to enhance our spirit and bring balance into our lives.

It was pointed out that if our reaction to those who acted badly against us was anger or resentment, we would have lowered our own vibration to the point where it could do us harm. We could become depressed, ill, or even retard spiritually. Instead we should endeavour to understand why the other person acted as he did. Ron's guide told us that it was not intended that in every instance we should literally turn the other cheek. He suggested that we have another cheek and therefore there is another side to the problem and a review of that problem may bring it forward in a totally different light. He asked us to accept without question that difficult experiences are necessary for our spiritual growth.

We were constantly reminded of the necessity to get to know and understand ourselves and our motives. It was not presented as an easy task. Any true understanding requires complete honesty from our innermost being but we are very good at making excuses for ourselves and we often seek to lay blame elsewhere. In fact to be other than honest is to our detriment and cheats nobody but ourselves. It is only by recognising and acknowledging the true motives behind our thoughts and actions that we can make any sort of progress along our pathway. The stumbling block is our own Ego and our refusal to see ourselves as we really are. Such aims are not achieved overnight, neither are they achieved in months. It takes years of honest introspection during which time we should strive to live to our highest potential in spiritual terms.

Importantly, it is our duty to protect our spiritual selves by practising forgiveness and not indulging in acrimony and other debilitating thoughts and emotions that retard our progress. Envy and jealousy often creep up on us when we are off guard and it is useful to know that we can help ourselves by avoiding contentious and vexatious people who would lower our vibrations.

It was Ron who first grasped the unimportance of some of the things we might normally allow to upset us. It is natural to be disappointed by people and events that don't turn out as we would wish. And from time to time we are irritated and bothered by happenings that upset our plans, but looked at against the scale of eternity our moods are often caused by trivialities which should not be allowed to upset us.

Our aim should always be to try and cultivate a calm, even existence. One where we make the most of the circumstances in which we find ourselves. If our surroundings are not to our liking and it is impossible to do anything about it, we should rest upon God safe in the knowledge that change will come and our present circumstances will pass.

It is good to recognise that we all have one thing in common although it may be buried deep within our soul consciousness and not evident to us through our intelligence. It is that the soul's basic desire and motivation is to progress ever forward and upward through all its planes of existence. It is as natural as the acorn's inward motivation to become a fully grown oak. But we can only start to progress if we look squarely at ourselves and recognise our strengths and weaknesses.

Without deep thought we may regard ourselves as being good, kind, fair and generous, but can we be sure? Each of us seeks to justify our actions but may be deceived by pride and Ego, or even lack of self-esteem. But a careful, honest review of each days activities will reveal us to ourselves. The real test lies in examining our motives for what we have said or done. Can we honestly say that we have acted unselfishly? Are we, even subconsciously, looking for some form of recompense for a seemingly generous action? Are we presenting ourselves to ourselves and to others in a false light? Motive is everything and self-awareness gives us the opportunity for self-improvement.

Realising this I decided to undertake nightly introspection with the intention of trying to be honest and critical with myself. The thought took root that I need not continue to be quick tempered and hasty, although as a child I had always been impatient and if it was irritating to other family members it was always soon over without lasting rancour. Furthermore, neither should I be intolerant and impatient with those slower than myself. I did not bear grudges and my flashes of irritation soon passed and were forgotten, but I was aware that others on the sharp end did not recover so quickly. The pace of my hectic life was fuelled by nervous energy and pondering on this, it became apparent that an inward change to be more patient and kind was not only desirable but that I would not have to strive alone. I could reach out to those in the spirit world for their help and guidance. Heartened by this thought I prepared to take another step along the way.

Through the work in our circle I had become aware of the guides around me but was mystified when mediums visiting the church told me of a young girl who was close to me. I was unaware of her and had not seen her in meditation, but when I met her in a dream she was every bit as beautiful as had been described. When I awoke I was immediately able to paint her portrait in which her long blonde tresses were bedecked with delicate flowers of every hue; the picture which today stands by the desk where I am working.

In the dream – which occurred twice – we were both dressed in long flowing white robes, and I was flying with her over a desert where the sand rippled in soft pastel shades of blue, pink and green. Flying was effortless and seemed perfectly natural. My companion and I were in complete accord until she drew ahead and I found myself lagging behind. I called to her to wait for me, but she said "Not yet. Not yet." And I awoke completely relaxed, marvelling at the happiness she had brought to me. A visiting medium told me that she had attached herself to me to learn - although I could not think what that might be. But whenever I thought of her and mentally asked for help, peace and happiness washed over me.

In this same period, my offices occupied the first floor of a building that had once been a private school and I had a delightful room overlooking an old but neglected garden. One early summer afternoon I was attracted to the mock orange tree which grew up to the open window and was savouring its heady perfume, when out of the corner of my eye I sensed a movement and a small hand protruded from the top of my desk. I stretched out my arm and gently took the warm, soft hand in mine. Behind the hand appeared the lovely face of a young girl with brown wavy hair and dark eyes that were looking directly and smilingly, at me. Time stood still, although it was probably only a few minutes before the hand withdrew and she disappeared. But that short time was magical in which the little girl and I seemed to exchange pure love. It was an emotional and almost holy experience that left me in a state of utter peace and happiness.

These young spirits appeared at the right time. By bringing such peace and calmness into my being, even for so short a time, they were encouraging me towards my goal and giving me a glimpse of how much richer a calm life could be. From them I learned that control of undesirable thoughts *could* be attained, and was heartened to persevere towards becoming a more balanced person.

However, having decided to try and break out of a habitual thought pattern was not quite the same as actually achieving it. I was still liable to be disappointed and impatient with someone who had not behaved as I would have liked. But now I found it possible to stop what I was doing, sit or stand quietly, and mentally tell my guides that I was more upset with myself than with the other person and did not want to feel hostile or angry. In asking for help, I was speaking to my guides as friends, and it never failed to produce an immediate result. It was always as though the anger or irritation had been lifted from me and a peaceful passiveness had descended in its place.

This was the beginning of an important change that helped me to develop an inward equilibrium until eventually a state of serenity and contentment took over my life. But it was not easily achieved and in any case, it was a long way ahead. At the time, the first important step was to face myself and acknowledge the need for change. Equally important was to acknowledge the need to be helped towards my goal. It was the beginning of a humbleness of spirit, a clearing of the decks. Eventually time proved that a change in spiritual character can follow, take root, and become part of one's natural being.

At all times, even in stress, calmness and peace is within our reach when we realise that we have the freedom to be exactly what we would aspire to be.

CHAPTER 11 - THROUGH THE VEIL

It had become a regular occurrence for us to spend time on the Lizard peninsular in Cornwall during the spring and autumn of each year. These holidays were arranged so that we could visit my mother-in-law who, with our help, had left the Midlands and was now living near Penzance. It should have been a therapeutic move for her to get away from the scene of so much unhappiness, but in spite of liking Cornwall and having friends there, she was still a bitter woman. Our visits were not enjoyable, and on my part, no more than duty towards my husband and daughter. It was a particularly difficult period in my life, when in spite of good intentions, I was constantly overwhelmed by the effect her mischief making was having on our marriage. Ron carried an unnecessary burden of guilt at having left her to live alone, and although he was hurt by the acrimony that always surfaced he never ceased to care for her. It would have been so easy for me to prevent us from going, but I felt she should not be completely cut off from our young daughter. It was sad enough that she had cut herself off from her other grandchildren by her similar attitude towards Vernon's wife.

Inevitably, over the passage of time, her health deteriorated and it became obvious that she was failing not only in body but also in mind. Finally she was unable to look after herself and needing constant care was confined to a hospital in Truro. On several occasions we had received panic calls when we would drop everything and dash down, always to find the emergency had passed. One Saturday morning, however, there was another urgent call saying she had suffered a relapse in the night and would we come at once. There was no question, of course we would, but we had had similar messages before.

Whilst the car was being prepared, it crossed my mind that this might yet be another false alarm and I thought I might try and see what the situation was. Sitting quietly alone I asked for help. Without hesitation there appeared a vision of her lying in bed. But most remarkably, her spirit form was hovering horizontally above her physical body. There was nothing else in view and seeing both bodies I knew this was a genuine emergency and her time was short and even as I looked her spirit was being released. We set off without delay and rushed down to Truro as quickly as traffic would allow on the old A.38. But we were just too late, which was very sad for Ron.

There was much sadness too, for his mother who in her lifetime had created so much misery for others and was the author of her own unhappiness. It was many, many years before she appeared at a healing session in our house and asked for forgiveness. She left with our blessing, and I remember the gladness we felt knowing she was making progress.

Since that time I have often used clairvoyance to determine the situation with regard to really ill patients, but it has not always been quite so accurate. Even so, we have always been privileged to channel healing energy that results in pain relief to a greater or lesser degree. Of course, there have been times when we have known that the physical condition is irreversibly deteriorating and all that is left is to give loving palliative care. It is then that we, as spiritual healers, try to induce an inner peace which instils in the patient calmness, peace of mind and even contentment. Under these conditions, during healing or sitting quietly, I ask to be shown how much longer the patient will be with us. Usually I am shown a tree from which I judge the month or season in which the person will depart. The only time this has failed is when I have misinterpreted the symbol presented to me, that is, misjudged the month. And it is a truism that a message is only as good as the medium's interpretation. I hasten to say that such information has *never* been passed to the patient or his relatives, but facilitates my under-standing of the situation and helps us when dealing with a patient's relatives.

Over the years my father had been quite dismissive of our visits to Spitalfields and had never seen reason to soften in his attitude. The family home in London had been bombed during the war making it uninhabitable and my parents, brother and youngest sister had settled in Gloucestershire with no hankering to return to the city. Indeed, they adapted easily into their new way of life, considering themselves fortunate to have been able to make such an undreamed of change in their lives. My parents were of the generation who had lived through two World Wars and were adaptable and philosophical people. My Dad in particular had great confidence in his own ability to cope with whatever life threw at him. He was a man of medium stature, muscular and quick in his movements. He was rarely without a ready smile and could see a funny side to most things. In later years his unruly blonde, curly hair became beautiful silver, but even in old age his smart, military bearing never quite deserted him. After years in the regular army he appreciated the warmth of family life and was devoted to us, and it could not have been easy when Mother and my youngest sister, Connie, joined the local Spiritualist church. There was a thoughtful side to his nature and he was open minded and innovative where modern technology was concerned, albeit a stubborn one when it involved the Spiritualist church. Neither Mother nor Connie could persuade him to go along and find out what it was all about.

There were times when visiting them that we would take along a Spiritualist Minister, Stan Papworth from the Midlands, who was booked to conduct the service at their local church. He got to know Mother, but had little contact with Dad. At other times when Ron and I visited, Dad and I would slip back into our old routine of discussion and argument and inevitably this led to talk of an after-life. Dad did not concede one iota and we would laughingly end with him declaring that, "She knows all the answers!" But that was as far as he would go.

It was sad that the effects of the First World War caught up with him and in his latter years he endured considerable pain from claudication - the result of frost bite in the trenches in 1914. But it was later, after he had suffered a couple of heart attacks that he asked us for healing. Another case of a person in extremis turning to spiritual healing when all else has failed! He turned to us more as a challenge than in the belief that we could help. He almost said, "Well, come on. Here's your chance, prove it." Importantly, he did not put up a barrier and was receptive to the healing energy we were privileged to channel. It was to his credit that he generously he did not attempt to play down the relief he felt, and readily acknowledged the existence of energies he didn't understand and had previously denied.

Some months after he had opened his mind to this new reality he was amazed to find that he was able to see his own guide, an Arab, a state of affairs he would once have derided. Here it is interesting to note that after suffering frost-bite in the trenches he had been transferred to Middle East and rode in the Egyptian Camel Corps. It was with pride that he had received a rare medal from the King of the Hejaz for his part in the campaign that featured Lawrence of Arabia. It was a period in his adventurous life that meant a great deal to him and it seemed to me that for him to have an Arab guide made the whole thing perfectly natural. And I must say at this point that I do think that often Guides chose to appear to us in a form that is acceptable to us.

The sighting of his own guide provoked a series of searching questions whenever we saw Dad and I was pleased that he gained a level of understanding so that when his time finally came, he had no fear of death. In fact three days before he passed on, he laughed as he told us that his Arab guide and others had come to his hospital bedside during the night, but Dad had told them he was not yet ready and to go away!

My mother agreed he should have a Spiritualist funeral conducted by Stanley, our Minister friend. It was a beautiful, warm, uplifting occasion and paid tribute to an honest, kind, gentle man who, outside of war, had never knowingly hurt another living person. It was only a couple of months after his passing that I became aware of him standing with arms folded, leaning against the doorway of the greenhouse, watching me repot geraniums. During his time in Gloucestershire he had become a keen gardener and it was so natural that he should be there with me. Now when I have a gardening problem I always say, "Now come on Dad, what do I do about this?" and then act on the first inspirational thought that comes into my mind. Let me add, with good results!

My Mother was a slim, vibrant person, black haired with expressive blue eyes. She looked more like our sister than our Mother! Her personality was quite different from Dad although they got along very happily during their fifty-one-year marriage and were always laughing together at the same small things, often quite incomprehensible to others. Dad was a practical man and, as the saying goes, could turn his hand to anything. Although an army man he made furniture, he built us individual crystal radios, and later made large valve radios on the kitchen table. Although for most of his working life he was a London taxi-driver, later in life he became an electrical engineer and worked for the R.A.F.

Mother, on the other hand, could be practical in an emergency, but mostly she was sentimental and lived her life ruled by emotions over which she exercised little control, declaring she could not help what she felt. I loved her dearly but have to admit that her life was made difficult when she allowed herself to be upset by trivialities and then let them rankle. Some of the important decisions in her life were made emotionally rather than rationally. She had a personalised notion of love, duty and relationships that demanded too much from others and often rebounded on her with self-induced stress. It was not surprising that in her latter years she suffered high blood pressure, hiatus hernia, bronchitis, asthma and arthritis, none of which were helped by her over reaction to life's little problems.

When she lay in hospital in a coma after a massive stroke, I asked my guides to allow me to know whether she would survive. Sitting quietly at her bedside I was transported to a huge cavern where I saw her crossing a footbridge that spanned the right hand wall. Below was a deep, dark abyss of unfathomable depth, but the opposite wall, from top to bottom, was lined with an Angelic choir surrounded by glorious light. Mother, entranced by the sight and sound of these heavenly beings was steadily making her way across. I knew then there would be no way back. But I could not understand the cavern. I disliked the dark depths over which she was traversing and it troubled me that her pathway had been potentially frightening although a firm, safe bridge and handrails had been provided.

It was some years after her transition that I recalled a conversation when she had told me that the most holy moment of her life had been at my naming ceremony in the synagogue. Mum said she had felt that she was standing in the very presence of God and his Angels as she offered me up to Him to receive His blessing. Thinking about it, it seemed to me, that the angelic host and heavenly music might have been what she had expected to find on her transition into the afterlife, and she would have been without fear. There was certainly wonder in her face as she trod slowly but steadily across the bridge.

The same dear friend who had conducted the service for Dad, conducted her service too, and those in the congregation who had never attended a Spiritualist funeral were impressed by his emphasis on the unbroken continuity of her life. Not continuing as someone who had been suffering so many distressing ailments, but renewed and once more in her prime. Nothing can replace a parent, there is always a void that can't be filled, but it was consoling to know that she was confident of an afterlife and I now believe she made an easy transition and had no difficulty in recognising her new situation.

In subsequent years I have not felt the necessity to often visit my parent's memorials in Cheltenham, knowing that no real, tangible part of them is there. I treasure the occasions they have been in touch with me since their passing, which are now very rare as nearly fifty years have now gone by. I just hope that I haven't been unaware of occasions when they might have tried to contact me. I will always miss them but I know they are alive and pray they are making good progress. And they are only a thought away!

It was exactly a year after Mother passed that I had one of my visionary dreams. In it, I found myself driving across a desert where the sands stretching out before me were the same delicate pastel shades as I had previously flown over with my young guide. The sky above was cloudless and the air was warm and clear without the slightest breeze. In the distance were hundreds, maybe thousands, of people walking diagonally across my path. It seemed that I was driving from east to west whilst everyone was walking north to south towards the warmth of the sun. As I came to them they naturally parted and I drove on until I came to where there were buildings. There I made my way unhesitatingly to an adjacent apartment block and went upstairs. On the stairs several persons were loitering but they didn't approach or impede me, indeed, I wasn't sure if they had seen me as I passed easily between them. It didn't seem to be my first visit as I knew exactly where to go and when I knocked at an apartment Mum opened the door. Tea was ready and we had a lovely, happy, chatty afternoon but of course, eventually it came time to leave and she said she would come down to see me off. The stairs had cleared of people and we arrived at the pavement to say our goodbyes. The beautiful glow of the tinted desert stretched before me and the sky and air now hung heavy in a golden hue.

Hugging and kissing her goodbye, I said "Won't you come back with me?"

"I can't," she replied ruefully, "I'm waiting for Connie."

I drove away leaving her standing looking after me and the vivid vision came to an end.

It was only a short time later when my youngest sister, Connie, had a heart attack. It was devastating. She was young - just fifty-one. A lovely young person with glorious soft, wavy auburn hair, and notably, a ready wit. Visiting her in hospital, it was a relief to find her sitting up in bed, bright, cheerful and her usual vivacious self. She was gladdened by the fact that the doctors had advised that her attack had been mild, choosing to ignore the rider to regard it as a warning not to over-exert herself. Being a church member she was well aware of much appertaining to our beliefs. So when I told her of my vision and that Mother had said "I'm waiting for Connie", she went into peals of laughter and said "I hope she waits a bloody long time!" Typically Connie! She found a joke in everything and it was wonderful to find her in such high humour.

Three months after she left hospital, Connie was lying in her bed at home when she saw the figure of our Mother standing by the window. She later told her eldest daughter Judith, that she was sure she was awake and had not been dreaming. Talking to Mother quite naturally, she asked "What are you doing here?"

Mother did not reply but silently beckoned to her.

Connie was stung into replying, "I'm not coming. I'm not ready yet."

Shaking her head, Mum sadly said, "You will be - soon." And faded into the curtains or the window.

It was only a fortnight later that Connie agreed to look after her four months old grand-daughter whilst Judith and her husband visited friends. When the young couple returned close to midnight, they found the baby had been fractious most of the time they had been away, but when she later settled, they had coffee and Connie went to make for home. It was then they found that her car would not start and it was decided to make up an emergency bed on a settee. Sadly, it was some time during the night that her heart failed and Judith was distraught to find that Connie had died peacefully in her sleep!

Judith was aware that her Grandmother had appeared to Connie, and also that I had told her of my vision when I had visited her in hospital. But I have often puzzled over the fact that I ever told Connie that Mother that was waiting for her! There had been no intention to do so when I set out for the hospital. I can only believe I was guided to do so, as perhaps, there was something important to be done before she took her transition. In the event, it was only after her own experience of seeing Mother standing by her bedroom window that she took steps to put her affairs in order. Perhaps there had been something on her mind and she needed to know that Mother was going to be there to meet her. I fervently hope and pray that this was uppermost in her mind and soul-consciousness when she passed so easily through the veil.

Judith has accepted these events as being perfectly natural, and we are both comforted to know that Connie was undoubtedly met by Mother whom she loved so much, and to whom, in life, she had been closer than any of her siblings.

CHAPTER 12 – LOVE IS THE BOND

It was great comfort to know that my parents and sister took their transition in the knowledge and belief that life is continuous and unbroken by death. Such confidence is held by countless others throughout the world according to their creed, religion or spiritual understanding, but is largely a matter of faith. Comparatively few are able to seek proof of an after-life, and indeed, many religions forbid investigation into such matters. Through our experiences, our little circle had not the slightest doubt of its existence, nor that we were in communication with those who had lived here before and passed through the veil. Naturally, we were interested in what we might call the mechanics of passing from this existence to the next. Often, when we were talking together or responding to a church member, we would come up against various questions "What happens at the point of death?" "Are we always met on the other side?" "Is there a heaven and a hell?" "Will life be the same as it is here?" "If I die through cancer, or any other illness, will I carry it with me?"

That we desired this knowledge was known to those dear guides who ran our circle and we were blessed with two addresses which helped to clarify our understanding, albeit they were delivered exactly two years apart. It would be presumptuous to attempt to paraphrase these communications as the essence could be lost in translation and I am therefore setting them down from recordings made at the time.

"17th February 1971 – communicated by Scottie.

I hope our evening together will help to bring about unison and understanding of things which are spiritual. It is our earnest desire that we may communicate with you to pass on to you that knowledge from the other spheres of which, at the moment, you are ignorant. But as one transcends from one state to another, one is able to communicate back again and pass on that which has happened to them. This is only the beginning, from infancy into junior, and we will have to contemplate that which will happen when we go forward into the senior. And this, my friends, is what we hope we will be able to communicate to you later on.

This is not easy as you have learned to date. It is a long and often tedious pathway because just as you have difficulty in ascertaining that which we are trying to impart to you; we in turn, have a similar difficulty in ascertaining the information that we wish to pass on from higher spheres. Consequently we have a long chain of communication all of which is difficult to actually communicate from one to another, down the line, to ensure that in fact, you do receive at the end, that which was imparted at the beginning.

It has always been one of the failings of communication when it is handed from one to another that it does become distorted, not necessarily intentionally of course, but in fact, as we pass the word mouth to mouth, mind to mind. Each opinion adds a little of his own mind onto that which he has received and even if it is only the manner in which he states that which he knew, and although it may be word for word correct, the actual meaning imparted of course, can be changed, and this is always difficult and why in fact, you do tend to get a great many interpretations of the same thing.

One will accept that he passes forward into the next plane and in fact, he joins his own family and lives on as though nothing has happened. This is perfectly true in essence.

But of course, one has to realise that there has been a change of state and that change of state has been brought about by the individual concerned. In other words, it was his earnest desire that he did in fact, re-link with those who have passed on ahead of him. Consequently his earnest desire was uppermost in his mind which he carried forward in his transition and so he did in fact, meet those he had loved and had known in the past.

On the other hand it can be the man who has gone forward who was not so concerned with his family, as much as his earnest desire to live more of his life and his life hereafter. Consequently he will not receive a transition in exactly the same manner. He will link with someone of a similar mind who is also earnestly desiring to live life and so we go on. But although they have both transcended from one plane to another and although those planes are very similar, it is not always possible for one to see the other, simply because he may in the first instance be completely ignorant, or secondly, have no desire whatever to know.

This is why of course, when the first man communicated back he has rejoined his family and his loved ones and everything is wonderful. The other man has transcended and has gone forward and he may have gone forward with a completely false conception of his own spiritual development, therefore, he can be quite bewildered when he learns in fact, that all that he has previous learned was of no great significance.

This is what tends to happen of course, when the people from the churches pass on, the ministers and vicars. They are good people essentially, but their conceptions are somewhat misconstrued as to what happens after death. Consequently, when they come face to face with the reality so far as they know it, on the next plane, then they are a little bewildered, and do in fact, have to reconsider and reconstruct their own ideas of what life was all about."

This address delivered at speed through Ron, formed the basis of our meditation for the evening. Afterwards, a member of the group wondered whom he will meet on the other side – his first or second wife, or both? And what might happen to a husband and wife when one is more spiritually advanced than the other - do they meet on the next plane? And Scottie intervened to say,

"For a portion of a time you will want to be with your loved ones so of course, you can be, but what we are trying to say is this. That because you are now developing spiritually and are obtaining a certain awareness of spirituality – that when you pass on, if, as we expect in the majority of cases, loved ones are gathering there to join you as you pass on, you will link with them, of course. But then when you have got into the run of things and have become part of the new home again, then you will start again to think spiritually. And this is where you may leave your family, just as you left your home tonight to come to this circle, so you will leave the family to go on to develop spiritually. They can either follow with you or you will draw away from them. The love and bond will still exist between you. It is not a severing off, but you will then start to go this way, but you will always link back again and you can always return back again. You will always have a bond with them."

Exactly two years later on 16th February 1973, a guide whom we called the Vicar, opened the circle with another aspect of transition into the afterlife.

"Once again we join together with the sincere desire that we, as we circle, may link with those from the other side who are of like mind and thus attuned to those of the higher spheres. That we may, by elevating our thoughts and casting the material things from our minds, form that bond which allows the meditation of those from the higher spheres to permeate through to us and give to us that which we so earnestly desire, namely the truth of life. Surely this is what we all seek? We read copiously of the various interpretations and yet we find no satisfaction because there is no clear understanding of the transition from one stage to another. If we could but come to understand that this transition is merely what the name implies, just a sliding from one state to another. Not a sudden change in dimension other than that which is created by the new form in which one lives.

One has been told that one dies and yet one is also told that one lives, this in itself would appear a contradiction. One must therefore put it into the right perspective. What is it that dies? Only the body which has been the vehicle for the spirit. The spirit continues to live and therefore in continuing to live, it must take with it that which it has already learned, and if it passes on into a new phase then surely it takes on a new garb while it traverses that new phase. Therefore we have the Etheric Body. This is again, only a means of transportation because we still have a great deal that we must rid ourselves of before we can become but purity of Light.

Consequently, as we traverse these planes we do so at our own time, at our own understanding and if we wish, can continue as we have done in the past, learning very little and gaining nought. Or we can if we will, study and ask questions and seek the truth and learn a great deal from those who have passed on that much further again. And because there is obviously a limitation on how much we can learn at any one time, until we have experienced certain new facets, we are not capable of understanding something outside the known dimensions, and this unfortunately, is where the trouble commences.

Everyone is willing to accept that which can be scientifically proved in the sphere in which they dwell at that time. Anything outside those known dimensions is ridiculed and said to be absurd. So it is unfortunate, because of this predicament that it is not until one has passed into this new sphere and experienced this new dimension that one can understand and appreciate its very existence.

Many have prophesied that someone will return again to the Earth Plane to try and explain once more of that which happens. Maybe this is so, I do not know. Perhaps it would be a great thing if it would happen, particularly if he were such as the Jesus Christ who came before, because the powers that he exhibited could have been put on trial at any time under any conditions.

Unfortunately, due to the materialism of people through many centuries, they have discarded the spiritual knowledge that they had, for the material. Consequently, the moment they are taken out of material surroundings they are unable to communicate in any shape or form, except perhaps, one or two who have the (mediumistic) ability. This is not sufficient to prove to science that a dimension exists outside their own, and so doubt exists and will continue to exist, unfortunately.

So you have always within your mind this doubt, this "is it or isn't it" and so the only way you can hope to achieve anything at all is to take it step by step. Learn if you can, that there *is* another world. That this is factual because in fact, you have been able to communicate with it. That it has certain dimensions outside your own that enables a spirit, once he has discarded this earthly body, to move at a speed quite unknown to yourself. That thought has a tremendous power quite beyond that which we comprehend. That these things which have been taken and accepted as merely incidental on the earth plane, do become more and more critical as one discards the necessity of the physical part of things.

And so, my friends, let us this night try and discard all that is material and concentrate purely on spiritual matters. That we may be privileged this night to link with those who have passed on ahead, who have studied and learned and because of their understanding would wish that those who will, may learn something of that which they themselves have learned. God bless you."

So there we had it. Love is the bond, the true bond, and it is to those we love that we gravitate when we pass over. We will not relinquish our free will nor the responsibility it carries with it, and in our own time, we will eventually pass on to higher dimensions as befitting our spiritual state. Thus we will continue our journey from one state of consciousness to another. Each new state requires a new vehicle to carry the spirit, each more refined than the last, until we become but purity of Light. Such teaching suggests a gradual loss of individual identity as one merges with like souls in the higher spheres. This may be beyond our comprehension, and even seem distasteful, but it is sufficient for us to understand that our aim should be to live this life in the knowledge that progression of the spirit is our reason for being.

I have referred to the reluctance of our dear spirit doctor to give us his name which he dismissed as being irrelevant, and not wishing to make the same mistake again, we gave our own names to our guides derived from their particular characteristics. It was not difficult to name Scottie who had a pronounced accent, nor the Vicar who always sat quietly, his hands clasped in prayer before he began to address us, and his manner of speaking was softly precise.

My own guide is the Arab gentleman who gives inspiration at all times and is often present at healing sessions. There is also a dear healing nun who overshadows me. She is a tiny person and when we are working together it seems that I have shrunk to her size. After any session when I have stood behind a patient, it still surprises me, when I open my eyes, to find that my head is not on the same level as the patient in the chair! My Guide Ephriam is a philosopher of high order and is working with me on the revision and extension of this book.

Other guides have come to the Group for short periods and we have named them all, one way or another! Our old spirit doctor who came to help and direct us at the beginning and refused to give his name, often brought others along to the healing sessions in the church and at home. "So they may learn," he said, "how healing works." At those times a healing session actually became training for those on the other side of the veil.

CHAPTER 13 – THE BORDERLAND

For many years I had felt sympathy for those who are suspended in the grey area between life on earth and the after-life. They may be souls who in their earthly life had no knowledge nor belief in an after-life and cannot imagine what has happened to them. Or they may be souls who do not wish to leave a person or a particular place, or for one reason or another desperately wish to cling to their former existence and refuse to recognise their new state of being. Whatever the reason, they are sadly lost and bewildered and can see no way out of their predicament.

My sympathy was put to the test when a number of us were invited by Mrs Harvard (not her real name) a medium very well known in the Midlands, to accompany her to conduct an investigation into some strange happenings involving two teenage sisters. A kindly, motherly figure she had spent many years serving the churches and was at an age when most people might have retired, but she was still full of vitality and good health. She knew us well as several years earlier she had given us additional instruction on healing and had followed our progress with interest. Excited by the prospect, we understood that ours would be a supporting role to supply additional psychic energy, but that we could participate if we saw or heard anything that might be useful. The chosen five were sitting in our development circle and hoped we could rely on our compatibility with each other, plus our closeness with our guides, to provide the strength of power the situation might demand. The medium, Ron and I were the only people in the group who had previously experienced a haunting.

We had little information to go on. Mrs Harvard had been recommended to a lady whose daughters were experiencing problems that suggested frightening ghostly visitations. We were only told that the girls' father was not happy that we had been called in and had dismissed the whole affair as nonsense. He wanted no part of it and declared he would be out of the house on the Saturday afternoon we were to visit.

So it was that we arrived in the small, ancient market town in Warwickshire on a bright, sunny afternoon and found the address we were looking for in a narrow pedestrian walkway between houses on the one side and an old Norman church on the other. The three storey house was in a terrace of similar old properties and in response to our knock we were given a warm welcome by a pleasant lady of about forty. She led us up dark, steep stairs to the top floor where the two girls had their bedroom and we found that they slept in a narrow attic room with a sloping ceiling and a window that charmingly faced the church clock. As we entered the house, Ron had seen the spirit figure of a middle aged man wearing a leather apron standing just inside the doorway, but he did not mention it at the time.

Mrs Harvard set a large tape recorder on the small table, plugged it in and checked to see it was functioning. We settled down. The mother sat on one of the girl's beds under the sloping eaves, but Mrs Harvard had said it was not desirable for the girls to be present. It was then that the mother told us of various events that had led to our being called in. It was alleged that over a period of several weeks various articles and clothes in the room had been tampered with. Some had been moved, some had been turned round, others were found in the middle of the floor and sometimes they had just been disturbed. The crux had come when one of the girls had the terrifying experience of having the bedclothes dragged off her bed as she slept. It was then wisely decided to seek help.

The proceedings opened in prayer. Almost immediately our leader became aware of the presence of a child who, she said, had a white apron over her dark dress and wore ankle boots. Unfortunately the child regarded us with hostility and truculently refused to communicate. It was very difficult and it took over half an hour of gentle coaxing before we made a breakthrough and she told us her name was Emily. Bit by bit we learned that she had lived in the house for many years, although she could not say when, and had been badly treated by her father who was strict and, she said, cruel. She told us that she was beaten when she was naughty, but sometimes she had been beaten but did not know why. She told us that one method of punishment was to be put out into the garden and be left there until it was dark which, from the way she told it, obviously terrified her.

When questioned, she said she used to be put behind a shed and she would pull up plants "To show 'im".

Then quite suddenly, she relapsed and again refused to talk, sullenly saying she did not know us and she didn't talk to strangers. We had to patiently start again, but this time, at least we had a basis on which to build a relationship. Kindly we told her that she did not have to stay in this house where she was so unhappy; it was not her house anyway, two very nice girls now lived here and she was upsetting them and making them frightened. But if she would go with the two angels whom we could see were waiting to take her to Heaven, we promised that she would be very happy. But this had the effect of making her angry and distrust us more. She flatly refused, saying that her father had told her she was too wicked to go to heaven, so she knew she could not go there. And anyway, she did not know who we were and why should she listen to us? It was very sad and seemed as though we were not going to be successful and would be unable to rescue her.

Then one of us asked if she had any friends and she replied "Yes, John. He makes shoes." She added that his shop was at the end of the row a few doors away. Ron then told us of the spirit presence who had met us at the front door and I asked Emily if she would trust John, who loved her, to take her away from this house and look after her. Pleased at the prospect of seeing him again she happily agreed that she would trust him and in the closing stages I was able to see her taken away by John and two guides noting that she was wearing a dark dress, white pinafore and boots similar to those worn at the turn of the twentieth century.

After a closing prayer and whilst we had a cup of tea, the mother told us that it had puzzled her that there was a patch of garden to the left of the back door where absolutely nothing would grow. And as we prepared to leave Mrs Harvard checked the recorder and to our dismay, found the tape was blank!

For a fortnight all was quiet and we congratulated ourselves that all was well. Then we got an urgent call to go back as Emily had returned as mischievous as ever. It appeared that the girls' father had decided to decorate the stairs and was working on the top flight when to his consternation and horror a roll of wallpaper was torn from his hands and hurled into the bedroom. It was he who demanded that we be brought back!

Emily was by turns defiant, sulky and apologetic.

"Well," she said, "he didn't believe I was here. So I showed 'im."

"That was not very kind," the medium gently remonstrated. "You know you shouldn't be here. And you promised you'd go with John and let him look after you. Why didn't you stay with John and his friends? Don't you like the place they took you to? We're very disappointed." And so it went on. Coaxing, sympathising, telling her how much we loved her until she warmed to us and trusted us again.

It was during this exchange that we learned it would soon be her birthday and a member of the group asked if she had ever had a party. Not surprisingly, she hadn't. It was then suggested that if she would be a good girl and go with her three friends to please us, we would have a birthday party for her. We promised that she would be happy in her new home and said we trusted her not upset the two girls again. We concluded with her leaving once again with the spirit friends and we went home feeling more confident that we had been successful. We had not attempted a further recording as we had now learned that it was not unusual for mechanical malfunctions to take place during psychic phenomena.

A few months later during a normal church service the visiting medium, who was unknown to us, said she had a message for five people in the congregation from someone called Emily. She said Emily sent her love. She thanked us for our help and wanted us to know that she was now very happy. A brief message that was so uplifting, and after the service we drank a toast in coffee to celebrate her birthday.

It meant a great deal to me to have been involved in this episode as for some time I had been assisting discarnate souls who came to our circle for help. They were usually distressed, feeling lonely and neglected and mostly unaware they had died to this life and were not visible to friends and relatives. Often some would appear in wheelchairs still experiencing pain or symptoms of disease unaware that their pain had no reality.

Being nearer to our earthly vibrations than those of the next plane they were brought by my Arab guide so that I could explain their true situation. My work was to encourage them to leave behind all that was familiar and go forward with guardian angels who would guide them into new, happier surroundings. I usually tried to demonstrate that they did not have to sustain their disability or illness by encouraging them to leave the wheelchair and stand up, or do something they did not think was physically possible. If that could be successfully accomplished they were more willing to trust that they could go forward.

At times the work could be disturbing as I experienced the pain, loneliness and bewilderment of the person brought to me. But I had complete faith in my Arab friend and knew that under his protection these conditions would be taken from me once the task was over. Sometimes rescues would be joyous affairs and easily accomplished and even tended to be regarded by the group as almost routine. The next episode however, was outstanding in the personal satisfaction and happiness it gave to me.

It was something like thirty years after the end of World War II when, during a circle meditation, I found myself deep in a tropical jungle. I was aware of thin shafts of light filtering down through the canopy and conscious of the dense undergrowth that pressed around me. With two hands I pushed and parted the thick undergrowth and tall grasses that were in front of me and was confronted by the wreckage of an aeroplane embedded in trees and barely visible in the greenery that grew around and over it. As I gazed at the scene the stillness was palpable. Not a breath of wind nor the whisper of a sound disturbed the heavy silence. The tail of the plane had broken off on impact, and I found that I had entered the main body of the aircraft and was viewing the interior.

There, in the silence, several young men in R.A.F. uniforms were lounging about in complete lassitude and boredom. They were as amazed to see me as I was to see them and tentatively, one by one, they got up and came to greet me. There they were suspended in time, aware they had crashed and still waiting for rescue from ground troops and in had walked a civilian woman! They did not know what to make of it and crowded around laughing and asking how I had got there. It was for me to explain as carefully and gently as I could that the crash had been fatal for them, but that nevertheless, they were alive and I was their rescuer. Not that I was alone for I could now see the shining guides who were waiting to escort the young crew to their new life and blessedly I was able to watch them leave.

It is an episode I have never forgotten, so vivid is the memory of their excitement and laughter when they realised that they had been released from their wretched situation and their eagerness to go with the guides was wonderful. My outstanding impression is that they were just young men, little more than boys. For thirty years they had existed in the borderland, suspended in a timeless vacuum waiting for release, and I had been privileged to take part in the rescue operation. It was one of the happiest experiences of my life.

We might wonder how people become trapped in similar circumstances to those just related. Perhaps the " borderland" is best explained as a state of ignorance between the corporeal world and the next plane. But perhaps the explanation could be wider than that. In addition to those inhabitants who may be ignorant of the possibility of an afterlife, there are others who are held back by feelings of guilt and fear the consequences, or like Emily, believe they are unworthy. Others may have died violent deaths and wishing to cling to the earth plane are unable to come to terms with their situation. Those who believe that nothing exists beyond this corporeal world may need loving reassurance and help before they have the confidence to face their true situation.

On the other side of life, there are spirit guides who have made it their mission to try and take these souls forward, but they are powerless when the soul is unable to recognise their presence. At times the spiritual light of these selfless beings is too bright for those who need help. It is as though they are looking into the sun and need to protect their eyes from its power. It is then that help is sought from those on the earth plane who understand the work and have pity and heart felt compassion for the plight of these unhappy souls. Regrettably there will be those who consistently refuse to recognise their true state, but ultimately a way will be found to save them from themselves. Eventually all will go forward, in their own time, which is incalculable in our terms.

CHAPTER 14 – HABITS OF THOUGHT

Heightened sensitivity becomes a natural part of our lives when we are in regular communication with the spirit world. We become increasingly aware that we are guided by those who have our best interests at heart, and experience teaches us that seemingly small events may have significance. It seems that whilst we have Free-will and should always be in control of our actions, there are times when we seem to respond in an involuntary way to spirit influence.

Perhaps this is well illustrated by Ron's narrow escape when driving home one evening from the Atomic Energy Authority's plant at Harwell. An escape which he attributed to subliminal guidance. He visited the plant every Monday and delayed his return home until the traffic had calmed and he could speed along at an enjoyable pace, which in his case meant fast! En route was a short steep hill that had a long, narrow decline on the far side of the brow. On this particular occasion, for no apparent reason, as he approached the hill he took his foot off the accelerator and gently coasted to the top. Imagine his incredulity when he reached the brow, to see a large articulated lorry jack-knifed across the road blocking his way! He always asserted that there had been no reason for him to slow up, the road had appeared clear, and yet he had responded to an over-whelming irrational urge. His action was so unusual and contrary to his normal way of driving that he had no doubt he had been well taken care of!

Recognition that similar, if less dramatic experiences, were constantly helping to shape our lives, served to affirm and strengthen our beliefs to the point where we took a step beyond belief, and let faith take over. Ron's guides often spoke of surrendering to the Will of God and we came to appreciate the futility of saying the Lord's Prayer and repeating "Thy Will Be Done" if we resented or questioned disruptive events in our lives, or the lives of others we knew. We found strength in accepting that there is order and balance in all things, and that even disagreeable events happen for our ultimate good. True faith brings contentment whatever our circumstances, and peace to our soul. We are able to regard material setbacks as a stony pathway, confident that a smoother path lies ahead. This expansion of consciousness might be expressed as being "In harmony with life".

It is not for us to see God's overall plan, nor claim to know the Truth, but it *is* our responsibility to seek to know the truth of our being. The group shared our faith, and together we made it our aim to return to the spirit world more spiritually refined than when we left.

We realised that we are here to undergo a lifetime of personal experiences involving countless spiritual and moral dilemmas, some large and some small. . It would be how we dealt with those experiences and the lessons we learned from them that would determine our spiritual progression. We also realised that although some experiences may be devastating and difficult, in reality they are more than just a testing ground, they are doors to wisdom and growth.

Not one of us is perfect. We are born into this life flawed and the circumstances of our birth – our parents, our environment or health, may give us a poor material start. But these circumstances should not be regarded as disadvantages nor hindrances to spiritual progression. They are in fact, the right conditions for each individual soul and provide the opportunities we need to make progress and eradicate those aspects of our nature which hold us back. Individually it may take us a very long time, even a lifetime, to identify and improve our spiritual selves, or it is possible that we enjoy and are content with being the person the Ego tells us we are.

In addition to parentage and environment, we come into the world burdened by various weaknesses that might possibly include selfishness, arrogance, quick temper or duplicity, etc in varying degrees. If these are not disciplined they become ingrained and a natural part of oneself. Furthermore, experiences and relationships along our pathway may cause us to react negatively and develop any number of other spiritually debilitating qualities. Accordingly, we might find that we have allowed prejudice, intolerance, hatred, mistrust, envy, pride, snobbishness, conceit, possessiveness, bitterness and desire for revenge, to become part of our persona. Or we may develop a predilection to worry with its direct affect on our physical health. Such negatives can manifest gradually without our being aware, and are all part of the human condition irrespective of our roots.

On the other hand there are souls who come into the world a little more spiritually developed and are examples of probity and goodness. They are to be found in all walks of life, and their light is a shining example to others who recognise their goodness through their kindnesses, consideration and the Love they generate. But even they may be vulnerable to self-satisfaction and pride if they regard themselves as superior. It is not often recognised that it is unwise to attract the envy of those more unfortunate than oneself, as this could contribute to the negativity of those who are envious by nature. It is also unwise to provoke ignorant persons or those of lower spiritual development to express themselves in anger, or in other ways that may retard their spiritual progress.

True humility of spirit draws respect and allows others to express their better nature. It may take many lifetimes to develop a refined moral character from which many flaws have been eradicated. Is it not incumbent upon us to be compassionate towards those who are still struggling with weaknesses we may have been blessed to overcome?

For change and spiritual advancement to come about it is necessary to seek to know oneself and recognise the importance that the Chattering Mind and Ego play in our lives. But we had not reached that stage of understanding in our circle as we concentrated on communication with the spirit world and development of our Gifts of the Spirit. But gradually we came to the realisation that we were changing and our perception of the world around us was changing too.

It has to be true that where there is conceit and self-satisfaction there will be no true introspection, no self-knowledge and no real advancement. Only recognition and admission of one's weaknesses and a strong *desire* for change can open the door to change. However, even the notion of changing our persona is daunting! We are comfortable with ourselves and cannot imagine being other than we are. Our friends, families and colleagues are used to us and our funny ways, and we are confronted by the thought that they may not like us if we became different.

But the changes we seek are for our betterment and by conscious control we are choosing to be nicer, kinder, more tolerant, generous and loving. If we can take the first step and travel a little way along the new pathway, we soon find that contrary to our fears, friends and relatives seem nicer, kinder and more loving *to us,* and people are gravitating to us and are glad to be in our company. We will never achieve all we set out to do as we cannot attain perfection in this world, but that should not prevent us from aiming high. The fact that we acknowledge the need for change and are prepared to strive for improvement, draws wiser beings from the other side of the veil closer to us, and we become more sensitive to their promptings and can take a long term spiritual view under their guidance.

Thought is one of the most powerful energies available to mankind.. Every action that happens through human agency is preceded by thought. Medical and scientific advances, our political alliances, the world we have built around us, have all resulted from thought. This is evident in connection with material things where planning and effort are necessary to bring an action into being. It is less evident with ourselves as we tend to regard ourselves as the same person we have always thought we were. In fact, what we are today is the fulfilment of our thoughts and actions in years gone by. And what we think today determines and shapes our mature selves and our tomorrows.

Habitual thoughts become ingrained and are perpetually recreating us for better or worse. To respond to others with kindness nurtures a caring personality. If we act unselfishly, putting another first, we will be caring. If we allow envy into our thoughts, resentfulness and discontent becomes part of our nature. If we allow anger to constantly erupt, we become quarrelsome. If we think fearfully, we may eventually become timid and withdrawn. If we think deceitfully we are not being honest and may become untrustworthy. If we dwell on revenge we become consumed with bile that reacts on our physical body. If we allow negative and unhappy thoughts to control us, we lose self-confidence and lay the foundation for long term unhappiness.

Conversely, if our perception of the world and those around us is positive and directed by kindness, compassion and tolerance, we bring harmony and contentment not only into our own lives but also into the lives of those with whom we are in constant contact. But it is impossible to attain harmony and peace within unless we can truly forgive those who have acted badly against us. It may be difficult to forget but it *is* within us to forgive and in so doing, release ourselves from the power of enmity and ill-will.

Repetitive thoughts create repetitive behaviour that for good or ill become part of our identity. To break out of the straight jacket of any form of negativity requires considerable effort and patience. The first hurdle is to recognise thoughts that are undesirable, and secondly, acknowledge that they impede our progress. For instance, we may need to concede that it is desirable to cultivate a more open mind because another person's ideas may be as equally valid as our own. This could be a huge step for someone who has always led the way.

At this stage of our progression we also understood the need to examine our motives for what we have said or done. It takes courage to face the truth of our inner being, but it is a worthy challenge. Honest introspection of ourselves also broadens our understanding of others. It helps us to recognise that everyone has qualities to commend them, and if we dislike something about them there may be other qualities that we can appreciate or tolerate.

It is when a familiar denigrating thought springs automatically to mind, or an unkind retort comes thoughtlessly to our lips, that we may realise how deeply ingrained our habits are. But if we sincerely desire to progress, it is encouraging to know that we are capable of the perseverance required to banish such unworthy thought patterns and gradually replace them with others that are more worthy. We are rewarded when these new ways of thinking gradually become a natural part of our persona. Getting started is not something we can put off until tomorrow or sometime in the future. The past has gone and the future is not within our reach. There is no time other than *now.*

The wonderful thing is that even in these early stages of our development we never forgot that we can reach out to those souls in the afterlife, who are closer to us than our hands and feet, and whose dearest wish is to assist our spiritual advancement. We ask for their wisdom, guidance and help, and we pray to God, the Almighty Power or Source, for strength to overcome our weaknesses. When we humbly acknowledge the need for help and allow this need to express itself, we open a door and create the conditions in which we can be influenced for our highest good.

Changes are slow, almost imperceptible, until there comes a day when we realise that we have naturally reacted to a situation in a better way than we might have done some years earlier. To know that our feet are firmly on the path and that progress has been made is a joyous realisation.

CHAPTER 15 – REGRESSION

Our understanding of death of the body is that it facilitates the release of the spirit into a higher rate of vibration within which it continues to function. The old physical body is completely discarded, but the etheric, or spiritual body, carries with it the mind, intelligence and spiritual understanding. The mind is still the same, it doesn't suddenly become wise and the personality of the individual is as strong as it ever was. The etheric body will carry the spirit to the level at which it is qualified to function, which will usually be the Astral plane, the plane nearest to that of physical earth. And we understand it will take many lifetimes to earn the right to rise through the various planes of existence. This was summed up by Jesus who is quoted as saying "In my Father's house there are many mansions."

Although the group accepted that we would need many lifetimes to actually refine our spirituality, we still asked ourselves many questions about how it could happen. We asked whether we might be required, or even choose, to live here again or perhaps, elsewhere? We wondered if everyone would return and who chose our circumstances? We understood that we cannot achieve spiritual perfection whilst on earth and it therefore follows that if we return, we still will not be able to achieve it. So, we asked, what would be the point? But our guides have emphasised many times, that this earthly plane is the plane of greatest opportunity to progress because of the experiences available to us and our gift of Freewill.

It is a strange quirk of nature that we often detect flaws in others, that are in fact a mirror image of the flaws in ourselves, although this is hard to digest and most people find the idea quite unacceptable. Tolerance comes with recognising that we are all on the same path, albeit at a different stages. Not on a ladder where some are elevated higher than others, but just a little farther along the pathway. Who are we to judge another's worth? Might it be that we have walked the same pathway as he whom we might criticise? Have we indeed, passed this way before?

When therefore, we were presented with an opportunity to explore the possibility of reincarnation, five of us decided to take advantage of what we perceived to be another open door. We discussed the matter carefully and concluded that our now long experience equipped us to take such a step. It was hoped that the outcome might provide a measure of enlightenment and perhaps enable us to identify an underlying pattern or motive for our present life.

It would irresponsible however, to omit from this record the warning issued with the material we used. Both author and publisher warn that regression is not to be treated lightly and certainly not used as a party game. They stress that unpleasant experiences have occurred when experiments were carried out in America and London, also in Australia where the system was devised. Special steps and exercises need to be rigorously and *completely* carried out before the subject is put into a semi-hypnotic state. Only then is it possible to induce visions of a previous life. It is not unknown for the subject to suffer extreme distress, or at the other end of the scale, extreme happiness. However, as it is a condition of the experiment that the subject must always be aware of his natural surroundings even whilst experiencing a previous life, he can terminate the proceedings at will. It is not my intention to encourage anyone to follow our example, quite the contrary, therefore I will not be giving the modus operandi, except to say that one person undertakes the task of "talking" the "subject" through the vision. He is called the handler, and his questions lead the subject into observing his surroundings. Obviously, as the handler becomes more accomplished the results are more detailed; but we had to find our way.

We gathered in a warm, well lit room in the comfort of our own home and set up a tape recorder. I volunteered to be the first to undertake the experiment and my regression was short and incomplete as it touched only a small part of that particular lifetime and didn't proceed into maturity. Let me explain.

My first experience came easily, but it surprised me to find myself as a young teenage girl emerging from a large, round mud hut in what I thought might be Jordan or Saudi Arabia. Balancing a bucket of sorts on my head I walked barefoot to a nearby well. My dress was plain, made of coarse

101

material with a thin rope tie around the waist. Looking to the right across an empty, rocky desert I could see blue mountains shimmering through the heat haze and my thoughts went out to my father who I knew was many miles away in that direction, selling the goats I tended. I was sad as I knew he would not be back for some days. As I neared the well I came upon some youths laughing and talking idly in the shade of a large tree. Feeling self-conscious, I lifted the bucket down, tossed my head and looked the other way to avoid attention. Having drawn water I then found myself re-entering the mud hut.

I noticed a small inner passage to the right which followed the contour of the outer wall and formed a recess apart from the main room. My attention turned to the room and to a young child asleep on goat skins that covered most of the earthen floor. I knew the child in my care was a sibling and as I returned to normal consciousness I realised my name was Yasmin. I was intrigued about that passage as I could not think such a design existed. However, one of our group was a sales director who spent a good part of each year in the Middle East, and he assured me that such a structure was normal and that the passage served for toiletry purposes.

I would have liked to know more about life as Yasmin but we were inexperienced and had underestimated the lengthy procedures that had to be completed before regression could begin. The whole session therefore took much longer than expected and disappointingly had to be cut short. It pleases me to know that at some time I have experienced poverty and perhaps will not have to undergo the same trial again. But I had felt very vain and vanity is still part of my psyche and I doubt if there has been any improvement. I am vain about my appearance and surroundings and doubtless my constant aim for perfection is part of the same flaw.

As their turn came, others in the group had widely differing experiences. There were varying degrees of success dependant on the subject's ability to cope with the difficult preliminary exercises. All their previous lives were quite ordinary according to the eras in which they took place, but nevertheless, seemed to bear some aspects of character which linked with their present circumstances. There were no extravagant claims to be Cleopatra, Julius Caesar, Marie Antoinette or some other romantic figure and this made the exercise doubly satisfying.

Ron had become adept as the handler, encouraging the "victim" to look around and observe his surrounding and express feelings and when his own turn came one of the group took over as handler. Quite unexpectedly he found himself aboard a sailing vessel en route for the New World. He was dressed in clothes reminiscent of the Georgian era that included a yellow silk waistcoat with a cravat and white breeches. He understood he was on board as a passenger having banished from his family in England because of his gambling habit. He did give the name of the vessel, but we were far too busy to check to see if that ship actually existed. Later Ron explained to us that he thought it quite remarkable because in this present life he would never gamble in case he couldn't stop! And he frequently wore a cravat!

By the time my second session came round we were used to the routine and results were more detailed. As I lay on the carpet in front of a warm fire, the last thing I expected was to find myself as a young boy of ten or eleven years old. A grossly overweight, really fat boy! The vision opened in a school playground where I was surrounded by children taunting me about my size and my ungainly and clumsy appearance. A figure of ridicule and contempt, cowering against a wall with nowhere to run and nowhere to hide. It was painful and distressing. I hated myself and I hated those who were abusing me. And as I wept in the playground, I sobbed to my handler as I described my torment and unhappiness. He then wisely asked me to leave the scene and proceed forward a given number of years, which I gladly did.

It was then that I became aware of a small dingy office and myself as a young man, quite portly, perched on a high stool entering figures in a large, heavy ledger. The office was sparsely furnished, only a desk, stool, wooden cupboard and a hat stand came into view. Looking round I noticed an old fashioned inkwell on the desk. Only a limited amount of light entered through a small dirty window which made the room dark and gloomy. No wonder I was wearing steel rimmed glasses. Glancing down I saw I was wearing a brown knickerbocker suit that tucked into knee length hose. When my handler asked me the date I could not immediately answer but took a few steps to the window and looked out onto the dismal scene below. It was early evening in winter. An orange haze hung over wet pavements along which hurried pedestrians hunched against the weather. It was obviously a busy town as the road was crowded with horse-drawn trams and carts. It came to me that I was in Germany, my name was Hans and it was before the First World War. I stood by the window sad and lonely and there was nothing more to say. My handler moved me on.

Moving forward five years as requested, my first sensation was of intense cold. I found myself shivering with an iciness that permeated every part of my body, although I was fully aware that in reality I was lying comfortably in a warm room. The realisation came that I could not move. My legs and lower body were trapped. I lifted my head and saw I was pinned down in deep mud by a dead horse lying across my lower limbs. I had no idea what had happened or how long I had lain there. Perhaps I had been unconscious. I only knew I felt very cold and very weak. Hopelessness and despair swept over me as I realised there was no escape and I told my handler (Ron) that I was resigned to the inevitable. Hearing this, he asked if I would like to go through the death experience and at that point I could easily have chosen to come back to reality. But feeling safe in his hands, I opted to go on.

Still reciting the experience as it happened and visibly shivering with cold, I told those in the room that I (Hans) was not afraid. My short life had been so unhappy that, in a way, I was glad it was coming to an end. I was not aware of the surrounding battlefield, only a cameo of mud, the cold and the horse. But the cold gradually lessened as numbness crept over me and the weight of the horse seemed to diminish as feeling left my body. I remember telling my handler how peaceful I felt. Then out of the darkness I saw bright lights bobbing just above the ground and as they approached I could see beautiful beings within. They came towards me with hands and arms outstretched and as I effortlessly floated out of the mud towards them I found they were standing in front of me. I looked down at my body still trapped and as they gently and easily led me away the scene faded from my consciousness.

There was no identifiable moment of death. No sudden sensation. Just a gentle, easy continuation of myself and a glad realisation of blessed release. It was a wonderful experience which has stayed with me and been of great comfort when someone I have loved has taken their inevitable transition.

The immediate link with my present life is my irrational fear of horses. I will make a long detour rather than go through a field in which one is grazing, even if others are walking with me. It is also intriguing that I share with Hans an interest in figure-work and am happy and relaxed when doing accounting. Conversely, there is no doubt that as an object of derision Hans suffered low self-esteem and self doubt and his short existence was a painful one. This contrasts with my present life where I am personable and confident, attributes which have given me the opportunity to earn the respect of others, something denied to Hans.

But most intriguing is my reluctance to visit Germany. I could have served there in the army towards the end of World War II but refused the opportunity, although some of my friends did go. Two or three times since then it has been suggested that we take a holiday cruise on the Rhine, but I have always rejected the idea, although I know it to be beautiful. Whilst not trying to justify this biased attitude, I have to acknowledge the influence of my father who told us harrowing stories of the First World War and my own knowledge of the atrocities of the Second. How could I not empathise with the victims of the Holocaust, knowing that if we had lost the war I would have suffered their fate, and although I can honestly say that I don't harbour hatred, I have the habitual thought that I could not be happy in the country where such atrocities, degradation and misery manifested.

Looking deeper into my life as Hans, and assuming that I had experienced genuine glimpses of a past existence, it is possible to recognise the Spiritualists' principle that eternal progress is open to every human soul. Normally this is assumed to relate to progression in the afterlife. But what if there are circumstances when as part of our progression, it becomes necessary for us to experience numerous aspects of human existence?

If this is so, it does not seem unreasonable that we should endure extreme conditions over various incarnations. In the experiments related here, poverty is juxtaposed to comfortable conditions, reticence and shyness against an extrovert and friendly personality, derision against esteem, and loneliness and rejection against friendship and happy relationships. To have value, the lessons learned in one lifetime must necessarily leave an indelible imprint on the soul's psyche and influence the lives that are to follow.

If from my regressions I accept the hypothesis that I have reincarnated at least three times, then it is likely there are other times unknown to me when I have experienced quite different conditions. It would seem that the sum total of these experiences is manifest within one's conscience and soul-consciousness. Hence the term 'an old soul' when applied to persons of innate wisdom, natural grace and high moral character. So much depends on how we meet with the adversities of each life span, the choices we make and what we gain from those experiences, and there seems no doubt that it will take many lifetimes to gain true insight and wisdom.

In fairness it is not possible to say with certainty that by the method we chose we were able to see into our past lives. But the small group who undertook the experiments were, without exception, convinced of the reality of their previous existences. Even now, some fifty years later, the lasting impressions are not those of dreams but of definite experiences. I am aware of what it is to be a poor goat girl growing up in a harsh environment and I am aware what it is to be mocked, friendless and alone although these conditions are alien to my present life where I am surrounded by love and know I am truly blessed.

The experiments that took place over several weeks, achieved their aim inasmuch as we experienced visions and realities of a unique kind and were satisfied with the results. In retrospect however, they were inconclusive inasmuch as whilst I know what it is to be physically and materially Yasmin and Hans, I really know so little about them. At surface level I am ignorant of their spiritual consciousness, thought processes and moral standards, although I felt entirely at home with their persona. But doubtless, within my soul I am aware of all that in the past has been of spiritual value.

CHAPTER 16 – A MATTER OF ETHICS

As the older circuit mediums retired or passed to the higher life, there was a scarcity of platform demonstrators capable of giving in-depth addresses on the philosophy of the Spiritualist movement. Many of those now serving were good psychics and often gave entertaining performances, but there were people in the congregation who wanted more than messages. In most cases they would have received one or more messages from the afterlife which they considered to be genuine evidence of survival, but they sought to know the implications of such communications. They were in the minority. The majority came to the services regularly and believed in an after-life and were content to receive messages and did not seek to know more. We found that if the minority who wished to investigate further were not catered for, they drifted away or came less regularly, having become bored with the format of service.

Something needed to be done, and Ron and I agreed to run a church circle for those seeking knowledge and spiritual development. We accepted ten as being a good number which would allow each person to fully participate and progress. As usual Ron's guides were the power behind our activities and he and I worked under the same spiritual umbrella. The circle had a fixed membership as we wished to build close unity and harmony that would have been unattainable in an open circle that anyone could attend. Harmony was not a foregone conclusion as people do not start with the same basis of understanding, and although there may appear to be compatibility there is often the odd one or two who spoil conditions by becoming envious of those who make speedier progress than themselves. And so after a little readjustment the circle became complete and well balanced.

Most had not sat in circle before neither had they meditated. We commenced by encouraging them to consciously relax by easy steady breathing and to visualise warmth and sunlight. They were guided to steady the mind, sit in the silence, find peace within and hold thought forms. We gradually progressed to the same format used in our home circle -

relaxation, a short guided group meditation and a reading followed by the main meditation. Thus everyone would be meditating on the same reading but what they gleaned from it would be reflected in their individual interpretation.

It was considered important that each sitter should be encouraged to interpret his own meditation in which he had clairvoyantly seen pictures, symbols or colours. Only if he was unable to do so or needed additional insight into the meaning of his visions, did I interpret with him. Listening to the interpretations of others gave members a wider base from which to understand their own visualisations. We made good progress.

Around this time we got very excited when two members asked us to conduct naming ceremonies for their children, one a newly born baby and the other a teenager. These could be officiated by the President who at the time was George, and he was ably assisted by Ron, the current Chairman. The format was as laid down in the Minster's Handbook and each child was given a spiritual name to add to their own and was presented with a small gold trinket. It was a festive occasion, and the committee decided to serve wine and cake to make it complete. I recall the teenager was given the name of Peace and today she is a beautiful woman; beautiful in body and spirit. Her kind and caring nature is particularly directed towards animals and a lot of her time is spent rescuing and caring for horses that have been ill-treated. It was a simple, moving occasion, a milestone in the church's history, and family members who attended were impressed by the warmth and easy friendship they found among the congregation.

But harmony is transient in this life of trial and experience and perhaps we should not have expected the happy state of the church to last indefinitely. In a quiet, unobtrusive way a new member joined who was to change the course of the church forever. To all appearances he was friendly, helpful and charismatic and it was quite some time before his dishonesty and deception became apparent. The first indication of his exploitation of the church's good name, came when Ron and I paid a visit to Charlotte, a long standing patient and friend, who was confined to a wheelchair with multiple sclerosis. She was living in a small three roomed flat that had been adapted to her needs and as is so often the case in such circumstances, had few friends or visitors.

We had been aware that for over a year, this man, whom I shall call W, had been regularly visiting our patient and several times had offered her healing, although he was not a qualified healer and consequently not a member of the church healing group. But satisfied that her condition had stabilised she did not accept his offer. However, we had thought he was being extremely kind when he planted shrubs outside her ground floor window.

On this occasion however, when we visited, she was very depressed and it did not take much encouragement from us for her to unburden herself. We learned that just over a year ago W had tearfully told her he was in serious financial difficulties and she had handed over all her savings which amounted to £2000 (a lot of money in the late 70's). She was convinced that she didn't immediately need it and the arrangement was that he should invest the capital for her and take the monthly interest to get himself out of trouble. However, a few months ago she had asked for the return of a small sum and although he had made many promises she had not received a penny. He had broken several appointments to see her and had now given up visiting altogether.

She showed us scrappy notes full of excuses as to why he could not get the money. The latest said the money was tied up for a fixed period and "the company" would not let him have it. Charlotte could hardly credit his duplicity or her own foolishness. She produced all the correspondence including his signature for £2000.

We took the paperwork along to a church committee meeting expecting them to take action as apart from anything else, W was also posing as a spiritual healer and a representative of the church. But we were met with apathy and lack of resolution. The Chairman who said he always supported the underdog, refused to support Ron and George when they declared their intention to confront W and ask for proof that the money had in fact been invested. But they went ahead anyway, and of course there was no proof! Under pressure W reluctantly admitted that the whole of the £2000 had been spent to pay off his many complicated debts. Ron and George insisted that he sign a statement to that effect and obtained a promise of weekly repayments. Eventually a substantial amount was recovered until W lost his job through selling "scrap" material belonging to his employer, and poor Charlotte lost almost £500.

In the interim it had gradually come to light that he was in the habit of borrowing small sums from a large number of people, and was in fact, still deeply in debt. Most people are basically decent and helpful to someone in trouble, but it was amazing to me how many who had so little themselves readily parted with their money.

The church officers were divided because of the Chairman's attitude, and harmony sadly became a thing of the past. Ron and I, George and Mary had over the years, meditated on the virtues of honesty, truth and justice, and were sure we had acted rightly. Others thought we were arrogant and high minded and not compassionate to a weak man with overwhelming money problems. In our opinion he was not only weak but also a calculating charlatan who was using the church for his own ends, and our sympathies lay entirely with his victims. We drew strength from the axiom that for evil to succeed it requires good men to remain silent.

The four of us were disillusioned by the turn of events and our regard for the church suffered to an extent from which we never entirely recovered. It was evident to us that there were committee members including the President, who regarded themselves Spiritualists but were in fact spiritists – believing in the existence of the spirit world but not aspiring to live by spiritual principles or values. In spite of their position in the church they thought our ideals too lofty.

After only brief illnesses, both George and Mary passed into the higher life, and then so too did Jane, leaving Ron and I without three of our dearest friends. Shortly afterwards Charlotte passed over, and Nancy soon followed. All were in their late seventies. We missed them all dearly as we had worked closely and amicably together for so many years and it was strange to realise that we were last survivors of the originating committee. I suppose it was natural that the idealism and keenness of the early days would diminish. Now there was no interest in holding large publicity meetings, and fund raising had become perfunctory. Slowly there was less emphasis on spiritual teachings and more on evenings of clairvoyance. The aim was to put bottoms on seats.

The problems arising from the W affair had opened a door and it was probably intended that Ron and I should have left the church at that point, but we continued to serve as before. However, only a year or two later another door opened to encourage us to walk away. We became aware that a church member was giving talks to clubs and organisations purporting to represent the church. However, she used these occasions to take bookings for private readings to earn an income for herself. We were also concerned about her use of tarot cards which in our view gave a false impression of spirit communication, Spiritualism and all the church stood for. But we were opposed by the President and the same persons who had supported W, whilst the rest of the committee remained uncomfortably silent. At one particularly accusative meeting, I gathered my papers and we left. I am not proud of it. But we were doing ourselves a disservice by continuing.

We were deeply disappointed by the turn of events but did not waste time asking ourselves or spirit why we had to leave the church. We had faith and we had our home circle. Others would judge if we were unreasonable in attempting to protect the good name of the church and uphold our principles. Doubtless our own attitudes and our reaction to those who were not in accord with us had played their part in the matter and perhaps we were not entirely blameless. However, it was now possible to recognise that for far too long our dissatisfaction had lowered our thoughts and vibrations so that we had been living in a semi-negative state – a backward step and hindrance to our expressed purpose to make progress. It was a time of immeasurable sadness.

At the time we had no idea that our departure would prove to be the catalyst for even more far reaching changes. For the first time in twenty-three years we had time on our hands to do things unconnected with the church. We began to enjoy life in ways we had not even considered and realised that whilst we had been so focused our lives had been slipping away. I set about selling the company I had run for twenty four years and a year later in 1985, we retired from the business world - and many more doors opened.

Some years later when the church had built its own meeting hall, a new president and committee invited Ron and I to be guests at the opening ceremony, and we were touched by the many tributes to our service to the church and healing clinic. It pleased us too, that mention was made of the sterling work and devotion of George, Mary and John – the latter, although relatively young, had also passed to the higher life by this time.

CHAPTER 17 – HAUNTING EXPERIENCES

We always regarded healing as the most important and satisfying aspect of our church work. It was a privilege to allow the doctors to work through us, and even at the end of a full day at the office we had never felt too tired to give ourselves over to three hours or more at the clinic. Now, although no longer attached to the church or healing clinic, we found that old patients visited us at home, and more came by way of recommendation. Others just arrived!

There was the case of Florence who had recently started to work in our house and confided that because of a chronic chest complaint her husband was spending all his time in an armchair, depressed and devoid of energy. She asked if we would pay him a visit. When we did we found him quite depleted, and his chest was certainly in a bad way and his breathing shallow. We gave these conditions our attention and also did our best to raise him from his depression. A couple of days later, Florence told me that there had been a surprising side effect on the night of the healing - they had made love for the first time in years! I almost expected that she would require us to see him on a regular basis, but she didn't mention it again. And I certainly didn't feel that I could!

We found that those who came to the house for treatment were somewhat different to those at the clinic. They had more need of counselling and we now had time to explore the underlying causes of their condition. The counselling usually came from Ron's guides during healing. But if we were having a cup of tea later, it would not be uncommon for Ron to be overshadowed by his guide who would intervene in the conversation to speak to the patient. This could be a little disconcerting when Scottie spoke in his broad accent! At other times I would be inspired to add to the counselling, so that we worked together as one. In this way we were often able to introduce our patient to the need for spiritual awareness and unfoldment. It is fair to say that never at any time did we discouraged patients from seeing their medical practitioner, emphasising that we were acting complementary to the medical profession and not as an alternative.

Whilst healing was our first love, the exorcism we had been privileged to do as in the case of Emily came a close second. We had been involved in other cases whilst still with the church, and felt that past experience and our knowledge of rescue work, qualified us to deal with a case brought to us by Joy. She had been a member of our circle since its inception, and had been in the group connected with Emily and she was still a regular member of the church's healing group. She didn't have a clear idea of the problem we would be investigating but judged that help was genuinely needed and we agreed to assist. She made all the arrangements and assembled three others whom we knew but had not previously sat with but we were confident we would make up a strong team and would be well guided and guarded. Furthermore, I was determined not to consider we had been successful until I had seen the troubled entity, if there was to be one, taken away by guardian spirits.

We all met in a pretty country town in Gloucestershire on a clear, bright summer day, and made our way to a building that had undergone an imaginative conversion into up-market apartments for retired people. We were met in the reception hall by a well groomed, charming lady in her mid-fifties.

"Hello there," she greeted us. "So glad you were able to come. I do hope I'm not wasting your time, but I really do think there's something very peculiar going on."
She hurried on. "This is the best apartment in the complex, and yet I can't sell it. It has the most wonderful views. Everything one could wish for. But buyers are just not interested and my staff are most reluctant to go up there! And I can't honestly say I blame them."

She went on to tell us that there was no disguising the cold, clammy atmosphere on the top floor and potential buyers could not exit fast enough. Nobody had seen anything unusual and there was no proof of a haunting, but she was a sensitive and intuitively knew that psychic phenomena was involved. Knowing Joy was a spiritual healer she had asked whether she knew where to turn to for help.

We were shown into the residents' lounge which was very luxuriously furnished and later as we travelled up in the lift, I could not help thinking how fortunate the residents were to be able to retire in such cosy surroundings. The apartment in question was a penthouse on two floors, and we had to pass through the kitchen to make our way to the sitting room above where a circle of six chairs stood ready. We were struck by the room's dank atmosphere and the fact that it felt much colder than below. Notwithstanding the large window and beautiful view, the room was distinctly uninviting. We joined hands and I opened with a prayer that we might, by the power of Love and Grace of God, be able to help whoever was troubled and in distress, and that guardian angels would be present and visible to us. We knew that without their presence we were powerless.

Immediately the prayer was finished I felt deep sadness and despair. A sob arose in my throat and spread to every part of my body. I wept in sympathy with the emotion palpable within the room. Holding tightly to the hands on either side of me, and drawing strength from the group, I shared the loneliness and unhappiness of an old man I could see crouched in the far left hand corner of the room. I could see his face and was able to mentally communicate that we were there to help him, and although I could not hear his voice, learned that he was lost and trapped and had no idea what had happened to him. He was distressed by all the building that had gone on around him and had no idea where he was. I told him that we understood and of our sympathy and love. I told him that he was lost because he no longer lived in this world, and that he actually belonged to a much happier place. I said we had come to help him and that he would soon be able to leave. As I spoke, two guides appeared in the centre of the room and reached out to the old man. He looked up, effortlessly arose, and without looking at us again went with them to the outer wall through which they all passed taking the cold, disagreeable dankness with them. It was remarkable how quickly the temperature rose and the room became warm and even brighter. Ron told us that during the time I was communicating with the entity he had seen several spirits standing around the outside of our circle helping with the proceedings. When we closed in prayer we were happy and elated with the outcome. It was a wonderful experience. So quickly accomplished because of the victim's desire to be helped and the power radiated by our spirit helpers. There were no further problems – one visit proved effective.

We enjoyed this work. It had such important purpose and achieved so much. We recognised there might be reluctance on the part of an entity to stay in the new unfamiliar surroundings to which they had been taken, and that he might return to the scene of the disturbance. Free will always applies. But we were always willing to make more than one visit to get a satisfactory result.

In all cases but one, we were blessedly successful. It was a particularly sad case involving a stableman who had caused the death of a little girl when he had set fire to a stable. The stench that accompanied this presence was horrible and most offensive, and at times the room in which he manifested was made quite uninhabitable. This was in spite of the present occupant being an officer of a local Baptist chapel who said daily prayers in the room. When we were called in there had been an unexplained fire in a shed outside the kitchen door and naturally the occupants had become very alarmed.

On this occasion Ron, Joy, Janet (the occupier who was a lay preacher) and I sat in the small room and the stench receded as we opened in prayer. I saw the man sitting on a bricked floor in a corner of the stable, dejected and alone. I also saw the young girl with long dark, curly hair, dressed in a high necked white dress, sitting quietly on a window seat in a panelled room. There was an air of resignation about her and after I had spoken to her and the time came to leave, she obediently went with the guides without a backward glance.

In contrast the man presented us with great difficulties. He was inconsolable and consumed with grief and guilt. In his anguish he could not believe that he would not be severely punished in some kind of Hell and was afraid to leave and face what he thought might await him. We made several visits during which we were able to communicate with him and although each time he agreed to go with the guides, and in fact did so, he always returned to the stable. It was most distressing for the occupants of the house who eventually called in a vicar who said prayers according to the rites of the Church of England. Unfortunately, this was not only unsuccessful but actually made matters worse. After a gap of three or four weeks the unpleasantness returned stronger than ever. The stench arose whenever the owners sought to use the room for whatever reason. It became more frequent and obnoxious until the room was uninhabitable. Finally the residents under deep emotional stress, were driven out and obliged to move away.

We thought that we had failed because we could not get together a group strong enough to deal with such a difficult case. Conversely, the guides had responded to us, and on each occasion took the entity away, so that ultimately one is led to the conclusion that the Freewill of the entity was paramount.

However, on checking data for this book it has come to light that after moving from the house, Janet discussed her reasons with an elder of the chapel to which she belonged. He told her that the land on which the house had been built, originally belonged to the Church of England who sold it for property development. In so doing they evicted a gypsy family who put a curse on anyone connected with the church who might live there! Unfortunately, Janet did not ask if there had been a fire or if a child had died. One could speculate that the gypsy's hatred and hostility against the church played a large part in the haunting. But there is no denying the revolting stench witnessed by many, the unexplained burning of the shed by the kitchen door, nor the two entities that Joy and I both saw. Janet later visited the new occupants and was delighted to find they were comfortable and happily settled without anything to disturb their peace.

Our experience has shown that only deep, sincere sympathy and compassion, without revulsion or fear, can be successful in this work. It follows that selection of members for a rescue group is critical. Motive is everything. A person should never be included for sensationalism or because he is related to another member of the group, or because he thinks he has a right to be there. That person may be more likely to draw and absorb power than contribute to it. A long association with the spirit world, knowledge of one's guides, empathy with others in the group, humility of spirit and sincere desire to be of service should be the criteria for inclusion. It might sound a tall order, but then it is not the work for everyone, and should not be undertaken lightly.

CHAPTER 18 – I AM

Just as we had found that our healing work had taken on a new dimension, so we also found that the teachings at our Wednesday home circle had become more profound. Our discussions after coffee ranged on often until quite late and our spirit friends stayed too! It was by no means unusual for Ron to be over- shadowed as his guides intervened in our conversation to add their wisdom to our conversations. Many times I had to remove his coffee cup or take a burning cigarette from between his fingers as he slipped into a trance and became quite unaware of us. These interventions were greatly valued and often the highlight of the evening. We well understood that although a measure of what circle members said was inspired, mostly they were expressing their own understanding with their finite minds. We were learning from spirit and each other, but from time to time had to be reminded that we were propounding ideas and thoughts as though we knew them to be the Truth forgetting that the whole Truth cannot be expressed, and is beyond human comprehension.

It may not be generally understood that philosophy and messages from the spirit realms, in translation, may become tinged by our mortal mind and our own thoughts and understanding. This had been pointed out to Ron by his old guide in the early days of our circle when he was still trying to come to terms with his mediumship.

At the end of an evening when he had conveyed a long philosophical address to the circle, he had asked, "How do I know that what I am giving off is really from spirit?"

The answer came, "When you first start in mediumship your messages will be 20% us and 80% you. Later as you progress the messages will be about 50% from both sides, and later still when we can communicate more efficiently is may be 80% us and 20% you. When it is 100% you will be on this side with us!"

A touch of humour much appreciated by Ron, and he never tired of reciting it. It reminded us that it is difficult for guides to get their messages across being dependent on the ability of the medium to correctly interpret that which has been given.

A further difficulty arises when we try to intellectualise spiritual ideas and concepts, but *true* understanding will come from our soul consciousness not from our intellect which at times may try to dominate our understanding. This was emphasised by the powerful guiding spirit of Ray, one of our members, who urged us not to be misled by the mortal mind.

"Which," he said, "is a collection of those things and emotions from within the mortal frame. Our brain is but an instrument which will decay and die along with the physical body. It is easy to mislead ourselves, to think we know a wonderful truth, when in reality we can only understand according to our awareness and spiritual consciousness. That which truly IS, is beyond the mortal mind." He went on, "One may read great spiritual philosophers and the holy books, but guidance will come not from the words but from the silence between the words. That is the way of Truth. Listen, read. Ask for guidance to understand the spiritual nature of the words. Greater understanding will then be yours. Only you can do it and whatever you learn you can only express to a certain degree, because that which you know from within yourselves you cannot pass on to another. That which is a feeling and a love expressed from within yourselves, from your own being, cannot be given to another. They must find it for themselves."

Our guides were telling us that we were only in the infancy of our understanding, and as will become apparent in this book, this was so. But I had come to realise that the Almighty God (or Source) to whom I prayed and who I thought of as being the mind, wisdom, power and energy *behind and in* all nature and the universe, and the universes beyond, *is* the living spirit, power and wisdom *within all* manifestations. An energy and many forms of consciousness beyond mortal imagination that dwell within all creation whether animate or inanimate.

I began to truly understand that man is more than a human who has a spirit, but *is the spirit*. A spirit being who is clothed in a temporary physical body made of the elements of the earth plane in order to live its life here. In the past I had often spoken to others of how the spirit that has animated the physical body goes on to live in a new dimension after so-called death, and thought I understood. But the full impact of the realisation that we can never be more spirit than we are *now* was an awakening! It was then that I understood the Truth of my Being. The truth that I am not the person I thought myself to be.

As God is the spirit, love and wisdom in *everything,* it follows that this must include me and every other living soul and I now know from the depths of my being and with complete clarity, that I AM a spirit. I am more than I ever thought possible in this lifetime or ever. But I am as nothing except as I am an expression of God's own spirit. The truth is that an infinitesimal part of God is our true self and thus we cannot be separate from God, although we may turn our consciousness away from Him. That I am part of God's spirit gives me all the strength I need and I have begun to release myself to the understanding that God IS, therefore I AM. I AM part of God and God in truth is part of my Being.

To be human (with a spirit) dependent upon the physical and Ego for growth and development, is to live in separation. We are the centre of our world and our perception of the world stems from our thoughts and the degree to which we allow our spiritual self to be expressed. But to BE the spirit with a physical shell to convey it through this life, is oneness with all other spirits.

Many of us are prone to allow small irritations to disturb us so that we grumble or even suffer unnecessary worry over everyday problems that are often blown out of all proportion to their true importance. If we are to progress we should recognise the need to protect ourselves from debilitating and retrograde thoughts. It is when we allow the Big I, the Divine I, to express itself, that we begin to create balance in our life and even the smallest step towards this harmonisation is a doorway to inner peace.

It is the mortal person, the Little I, who I later came to recognise as the Ego, who lets us down. It is it who allows our flaws and weaknesses to surface and the darker side of our nature to show itself. It is the Little I who lapses into despair and asks why God has allowed misfortune to come into our lives. The Little I lacks faith in anything outside of itself and cannot see the whole picture. It is the Divine I who has the spiritual strength to trust that everything that happens is for our ultimate good and that we are always in the right place at the right time.

It is proper that in this lifetime we should put to good use the intelligence, gifts and skills we inherited at birth or have acquired through study and diligence. It is also proper that we make the most of our material opportunities, providing that we are not harming others by the way we attain them. At the end of the day, all our earthly ambitions and all our material achievements assume their real importance when we have the insight to realise that our true success will ultimately be measured by the extent to which we have gained knowledge of the I AM within, and allowed it to express itself. This can only be achieved through a higher level of consciousness when we will be released from the Little I we once thought we were.

Recognition that God, or the Source, as the centre of our being gives us the opportunity to appreciate that He is also the centre of every other being. We are all souls on the great pathway although at different stages of understanding and we are united in spirit. It is some two thousand years ago that St. Paul so succinctly said, "Now there are diversities of gifts, but the same Spirit. And there are diversities of operations, but it is the same God which worketh in all."

CHAPTER 19 – TRANSITION

I stood at the kitchen window watching Ron trudge up the garden to empty a box of lawn cuttings and, once again, could not help noticing how slowly he moved. In his youth he had been a keen walker and runner, and for many years we had been dancing at least once a week, but his tall, slim figure was now stooped and thin - his vitality gone. Lately he had been short of breath and we had begun to sit out at dances. A blow to our pride! But there was no mistaking the change that had taken place and the fact that he had aged rapidly. Two years earlier our home circle had closed for what was meant to be a short break, but we had not reopened. We were not sure why, we only knew it was not the right time and waited for a sign to begin again. - but it had not come. At about the same time the number of patients for healing became fewer but when a case came the healing energy was a strong as ever.

We were leading a full social life, but it came as no surprise to those who knew me, when after a year or two of retirement, I was drawn into local politics. I had always been energetic and occupied in so many directions that I needed little encouragement to become involved in village matters via the Parish Council. It was at a time when there were difficult problems on hand regarding proposed encroachment of the Green Belt that resulted in two Public Enquiries, and it was interesting and fulfilling to steer matters from the Chair.

Although we were content with our life in the village, when I saw Ron dragging himself around the garden, I realised it had become too much of a burden and tentatively suggested we leave. He obviously had been thinking along the same lines as he unhesitatingly agreed although we had spent twenty six of the happiest years of our lives there. We thought we might move to a small riverside town, relatively unspoilt, and with all the amenities two elderly people might wish for.

The day after having our house evaluated we visited a small Georgian town in the Worcestershire countryside, where we hoped to settle; saw two properties and chose one that was perfect for our needs. We put our house up for sale the same day and within six days of having our house valued we had sold it and bought the other! It was yet another doorway, and if ever we were guided, that was surely the time! The move was painless, and with plenty of professional help we were soon shipshape and a small garden had been transformed into three easily maintained patios and a large rockery. Although it was not actually said, we both knew that I would be the one who would have to look after and maintain it and everything was laid out accordingly. Ron was enthused by designing and creating such a pretty retreat that his energy levels picked up and he enjoyed every minute of it.

The move proved to be exactly right in every way and there followed a year of contentment and happiness during which Ron relaxed and produced some of his best animal drawings. Then the Law of Cause and Effect from which there can be no escape, came into being and the blow fell! Most of his life a heavy smoker he had not stopped soon enough and we found he now had lung cancer and emphysema! He went through radiation treatment followed by a wonderfully happy summer, autumn and winter of remission. Then the awful invader took control again.

Our belief and trust in God the Source never wavered. Somewhere along the road we had attained complete Faith, although it had been a long road for Ron who had begun his journey as a die-hard sceptic. He had always believed in a supreme God, an unseen Almighty Power, but as a young man had scorned the concept that we might live on after death. It had been through his ability to channel such wonderful healing that he had advanced to the deep conviction that unseen helpers and an after-life actually do exist.

Our faith was strong. Faith in the existence of an omnipotent power of whom we are part and who is part of us. Faith that we are spiritual beings in transition. Faith that the only substantial thing about us is our indestructible spirit and Faith in life eternal. When talking to others about the afterlife, with wry humour Ron would say, "I *know* it is true. If I am right, you won't know. If I am wrong, I won't know." But he was right and he did let us know!

We spent Christmas 1997 in the countryside with our daughter and family, but it taxed his strength and he knew he would not make the journey again. His decline was rapid and it was pitiful to see him become a shadow of his former self. He did not complain but from time to time when he was really uncomfortable, he asked for relief which blessedly, I was able to channel. Quite suddenly he was taken into hospital and although I visited every day I was unable to see a consultant or doctor. On the sixth day I sat down quietly at home and asked to be shown how long it would be before he would take his transition. In response I was impressed with a picture of the plum tree in our garden and concluded he would leave in August when it would bear fruit. It was now March.

On the eighth day I was able to see a consultant who confirmed my worst fears that Ron only had a short time to live and suggested the next step would be a hospice. I told him my preference would be for him to come home where I had already made provision and could get assistance with nursing care. When I suggested that the situation might go on until August, he replied, "No. Some months, but not as long as that." I told him that if Ron got to know the cancer had returned, he would not wish to live, but even I did not really realise the strength and implication of what I was saying. Later that day Ron said how wonderful the nurses were and asked me to bring them some chocolates.

He was very quiet and lethargic the following day when I put the chocolates in the nurses' rest room. A young Houseman was doing his rounds on the ward and I suggested to him that Ron was under deeper sedation than the previous day and he agreed that tomorrow the drugs would be administered in smaller doses. I took the opportunity of checking on Ron's condition and was told that he had weeks to live. I told him too, that if Ron knew the cancer had returned he would not wish to live.

Ron had said very little to me that day, but suddenly he called the Houseman, and in a strong voice asked him the pertinent questions. "What is wrong with me? And how long will I be here?" The doctor started to explain that sometimes cancer returns but before he could finish Ron closed his eyes and sank back into the pillows. He did not speak again and at six o'clock I kissed him and drove home before it became dark.

The same evening – just before ten o'clock, a nurse 'phoned me. Out of the blue she said, "Ron says he's going to die and he wants you to hold his hand."

Stunned, I phoned our daughter and then a taxi, but the nurse immediately 'phoned again to say she was coming to pick me up. I presume Ron had told her that I had not driven in the dark since recently having had two cataract operations. I don't remember much about the journey. I think I chatted inanely. I know I asked if she thought he was going to die and she replied that she didn't know. But when we got to the hospital she dashed out of the car saying we might be too late. I was in a turmoil as we ran down the corridor and suddenly, in the half light, I was faced by the bed which only four hours earlier I had left in a well lit ward, but was now enclosed in curtains. I looked in to see a nurse sitting holding his hand, and as I took her place he started to whisper the most wonderful and loving things. Words too precious to repeat, but which I hear over and over again in his soft, sweet voice.

"Ron," I asked through my tears, "why are you doing this?"

"I am only going a little way down the road," he reassured me. "you know what it is all about." Then he added, "I'll never leave you, not in this world nor the next."

He denied he was being brave and courageous, and simply whispered "Not at all. I am happy and content to go."

Not wishing to disturb his peace of mind and to help him make a quiet transition, I sat holding his hand until our daughter and son-in-law arrived at midnight. At first he did not recognise them and asked who they were, but after greeting them he again relapsed. Sometime later, when his pulse was erratic and weak, he raised himself up and grinning broadly, waved towards the bottom of the bed.

"Who is it?" I asked.

"Ron and what's his name."

He never could remember Bill's name. When in the past he had spoken of them, his old teenage friends were always "Ron and what's his name."

125

He was so pleased to see them, and I put my head down onto his arm and prayed in thankfulness. Time passed.

Suddenly I was aware that I was flying above a car that was swiftly making its way down a winding road. I knew Ron was inside. I kept pace with it from above as it wound its way through patches of bright sunlight and then into areas of shadow cast by trees on either side. We were travelling together. A tunnel appeared ahead and part of me thought "We'll go in and see a bright light ahead." But even as the thought entered my head, I was pulled up at the entrance and was not permitted to go any further. He went on and it was perhaps, some twenty minutes later that his weary body drew its last breath. When we left the hospital in the clear, grey light of dawn, a blackbird's song filled the chill morning air

I knew from the outset that his passing had been a blessing. He hated the indignities of hospitalisation. But the final part of his illness had been brief, and his stay in hospital only a matter of days. Blessedly he had been spared much of the pain and agony associated with his condition. His passing had been as he had lived, quiet, gentle, dignified and full of concern for me. He was a man of utmost integrity, one of nature's gentlemen and it was a privilege to have shared my life with him.

His cremation was conducted by a Spiritualist Minister from Coventry. A lovely lady, sincere, sensitive and compassionate with whom I found instant empathy. It was a wonderful service during which she presented me with four roses drawn from the wreath on his coffin and twenty years later three of the dried flowers still survive in a vase here in my sitting room! When I returned home from the service I saw that the plum tree was in full and radiant blossom.

CHAPTER 20 - AFTERMATH

Ron made his transition at the end of March and on 1st June, just two months later, two friends and I visited a Spiritualist church where we were totally unknown. The medium proved to be a gifted young man who at the very beginning of his demonstration of clairvoyance was almost overwhelmed by Ron. Through him Ron gave the names of people he had newly met, including my sister Connie and our dear friend Viv. He came through in the company of a boxer dog which was an excellent identification as for over 12 years we had bred and shown the breed and were extremely attached to them. I was startled when the medium said I should get out Ron's diamond ring. I had completely forgotten that he had put it away when his fingers had become too thin for him to wear it. But now I wear it continuously and am comforted by the psychometric warmth and comfort it generates.

The medium went on at length to convey messages about other private and evidential matters. He was an excellent channel, but admitted to being puzzled by Ron's reference to a thunderstorm. It was a long message that came over with strength and enthusiasm and Ron was obviously delighted to be able to come through. I think he would have gone on and on, but the medium said he had to break away to allow other spirit communicators to come through.

Later I was able to tell the demonstrator that at the crematorium, after the large congregation had packed into the chapel and the coffin was about to be unloaded from the hearse, there had been a sudden tremendous clap of thunder seemingly right overhead. Afterwards I was told that it had amused those inside the chapel who had jested knowingly, "That's Ron - letting us know he's here." In fact, the thunder was immediately followed by a heavy deluge that heralded the floods that swept through the south Midlands in April 1998.

After his passing there came a feeling of deja vu as though I had stepped back over 50 years to the early days of our marriage and was again living my life in the slow lane, dragging out the days waiting for him to come back from overseas. Fifty-four years of marriage to one person is a very long time and reality only came gradually. I drew on my confidence and faith that death is part of a natural cycle, and that rebirth follows as surely as spring follows winter. My strength came from knowing that our separation was only one of blindness on my part as I knew he was often around me and there was the added comfort of knowing that on his transition he had discarded his diseased shell and laid down the burden of his physical being.

Seemingly we were two different sorts of people. He slow, thoughtful and reserved, myself quick, intuitive and outgoing but we soon found common ground. In later life he became disillusioned with new age morality and society, lamenting the loss of traditional standards and values. I would like to think that I have grown more tolerant, not only with age, but also by appreciating that society must change with each new generation.

When, however, it came to our innermost understanding and faith in the unbroken continuation of life, there was absolutely no difference between us. We had been fortunate to have spiritually evolved and progressed together. We were two sides of the same coin; blessed to have found each other in this lifetime, or had it all been part of some grand plan that we should come here to support each other?

Of course I miss him and realise I am no longer the first person in anyone's life, but self-pity would be self-indulgent and non-acceptance of Divine Will. There is still so much to be grateful for with good health, spiritual strength and spiritual guidance topping the list. Every day I thank the powers above for the sensitivity that allows me to be aware of his loving presence. He is often with me and always when I am channelling healing. There was an occasion when it was wonderful to see him kneeling on the opposite side of a patient and ministering in his usual way. At other times, his hands have closed over mine and I have felt a surge of healing energy. When I caught a brief glimpse of him sitting in an armchair he looked twenty-five years younger! His spiritual presence around me was close and real for many, many years. Now, 20 years on, I only occasionally feel his presence – often at the most unexpected times.

In retrospect I refer back to our Army days and a poet friend who penned a poem to us called The Two Friends in which he described Ron as 'The one who purely mirrors good', and it was this touching tribute that I had engraved on his gravestone for the world to see.

Recently when I was looking through his drawing materials I found two slips of paper on which he had written:

What is Faith?

Faith is the substance of things hoped for,

The evidence of things not seen.

I rest in God today – and let Him work in me

and through me, while I rest in Him in quiet

and perfect certainty.

I do not feel the need to attend church services, but on the odd occasions when I have done so, communications have been strong, long and evidential. On several occasions Ron has appeared to Pam who commenced her training in our home circle and for many years was an international medium. She saw him when she was demonstrating in Australia and said he was delighted to be "working", which we both took to mean healing. There have also been occasions when Joy too, has been aware of his nearness while she also has been healing.

Forty years ago, the night before the younger of our two grandsons was born, Ron and I were talking with our daughter and her husband about the coming event, when the Vicar overshadowed Ron and joined the conversation. He told us that the child to be born was a very special soul and of the mixed emotions that were accompanying his birth. There was, he said, sadness in the upper realms at his departure, although gladness too, that he was about to take a special journey. The Vicar concluded by saying that when "his instrument" (Ron) progressed to the other side of life, his gifts would pass to our daughter.

During the summer of 1998 a few months after Ron's passing, my son-in-law was walking in rough countryside and chose a path covered in loose shale. For some reason he was not wearing suitable boots and he fell breaking his leg above the ankle. It was a serious accident for such a heavily built man and of course he received hospital treatment, but recalling the prophecy, our daughter placed her hands over the injuries and asked her Dad to help. Both she and her patient immediately became aware of the heat and healing vibrations that emanated from her hands. She continued to give healing sessions and from the speed of his recovery it is possible to say that blessedly, she too is a natural channel to relieve pain and promote healing.

And so doors continue to open.

CHAPTER 21 – THE 4th DIMENSION

It was through a series of remarkable synchronicities that ten years later I found myself leading a new group of people seeking to be Healers. During that time I had sorely missed hands-on healing and the satisfaction of working in a group. I had asked spirit so many times that a Healing Group might manifest although I had no idea how it could possibly happen, but obviously the time had not been right.

But I had not been idle. I had written and published "Many Doors" in 2000/2001 which was an absorbing exercise and a wonderful release. The writing gave me an opportunity to review my life and decide what I wanted to do for the rest of it. And of course, top of the list was the opportunity to restart healing. It had been such a privilege to work with the spirit doctors, and I felt I had so much still to give, but although I had met and found good friends among the local ladies, there was no-one who shared my outlook on life. And so although we had frequent holidays and outings and enjoyed the theatres at Malvern and Birmingham, deep down I felt unfulfilled.

Since Ron's transition I had explored many theories and subjects to widen my understanding of what exactly is meant by spiritual progression, and had become aware of the influence of the Ego and the Chattering Mind that is the Ego's voice. I now realised the need to subjugate the Ego, which although a vital part of being Human, has become too powerful and controlling. The Ego promotes selfishness, ruthlessness, criticism, derision and intolerance (among other negatives) and is often the biggest obstacle to good relationships and spiritual development. In primitive man the Ego's task was to protect us from danger and it used "flight or fight" as weapons and they worked very well. But evolvement over thousands of years has meant that now the Ego urges us to be a singular person who is always better than others. Some Egos are constantly on the defensive and often presume attacks or slights where none exist. Other times the Ego urges us to lash out when it regards its pride has been hurt, or it thinks someone has caused it suffering in some real or imagined way, and it is often the barrier to loving and kindly relationships. Part of our separateness is to judge others from our own imperfect perspective. It is to our shame that part of normal gossip is to criticise others or maybe even deride them and think of them as inferior if they differ from us in some particular way. On the other hand the importance of the Ego is that it can be our strength when it gives us the confidence and self-esteem to assert ourselves to gain something for our true betterment.

In politics and religion the individual Ego and ultimately the Collective Ego, have deadly influence on the Peace of the world - often at the root cause of power struggles and conflicts. And the stronger the Ego of a country's leader, a religion or the patriotic fervour of a country, the wider is the separation between it and all others.

The disturbances caused by the Chattering Mind are like running water that cannot be turned off. The flood of thoughts are sometimes so over-whelming they can be quite disturbing and we long for a tap to shut them off. However, it was through the writings of Eckhart Tolle (A New Earth) that I came to realise that we can only ever live in the present moment – in the NOW. That is the only time in which we have control and the state of our happiness lies within it. We always enjoy remembering the fun and good times and the nice people we have known in days gone by, but often unpleasant reminders of the past intrude into our thoughts and should not be held there - and certainly not mulled over. We should note such thoughts as they arise and let them flow out without engaging them. Why relive disturbing episodes all over again? What has happened has happened and is beyond mortal change. Equally, our supposition about what might happen in the future is also futile as we find ourselves crossing bridges that aren't even there. Eventually, I really understood that we can only ever live in this Now moment and that understanding opened the door to an inner calming and contentment - and that is why I often light-heartedly quote:

Yesterday is history,

Tomorrow is a mystery,

And that's why today is called the Present.

My searching also led me to the concept that when we leave our Soul in the Astral Plane to come into a new earthly existence, only a part of us has the full physical experience. I learned that there is part of ourselves that we know as the Higher Self who does not materialise on earth but stays close at hand to guide and influence us through life for our highest good. We do not have a road map to take us on our journey and come to many cross roads with difficult choices to make. It is then that our Higher Self is on hand to give us inspiration and intuitive thoughts and guidance.

In the new weekly circle we had three main objectives, all equally important. One was to meet and get to know our Higher Self during meditation. The second was to draw to ourselves Divine Light and the Divine Energy of Healing to be channelled out to individuals in need of compassion and healing. On a larger scale the same Healing Energy was to be sent out into the dark places of the world where poverty, war conditions and misery exists. We also had an extensive Healing List of individuals who needed to be named for Absent Healing. Thirdly, I set about weekly training of three men to be Spiritual Healers whom, we hoped, would eventually open a Healing Clinic. To this end I opened my house to patients and we formed a good team and successfully dealt with a variety of ailments and conditions. Training the Healers extended over 5 years during which time the three also attended monthly meetings at the SNU's training class elsewhere. They successfully qualified and were certificated, but the Clinic never materialised although drawing on my business experience I had outlined a plan to help them started. It had never been my intention at my advanced age, to be part of the Clinic and it is one of my big disappointments in life that the motivation was not there to launch them on a new pathway.

I suppose it was 2010 when I first became aware of the Mayan Long Count Calendar. The Mayans were an ancient civilisation of a highly intelligent people who lived in North Guatemala, South America, and were remarkably advanced in astronomy, astrology and math calculations. They devised a complicated communication system of some 800 'words' and had over twelve large cities each housing tens of thousands of people. They also built very high red brick pyramids deep in the jungle some of which are still being discovered today. Their complex beliefs included human sacrifice, life after death and a fetish for blood. Importantly for us, they calculated that several long term cyclic cosmic systems would come to an end at the same time and the date they forecast this would happen was 21st December 2012. The Long Count Calendar covered 5126 years and the 21st December 2012 would be the end of their 12th bak'tun when the calendar would be reset to the beginning of another cycle – the 13th bak'tun. This date came to have diverse meanings. Many people are aware that the beginning of each new Mayan bak'tun had always heralded tremendous changes to Mayan history. This caused many to look forward to 2012 with dark foreboding afraid it would be 'end of days' and that some huge catastrophe would bring about the end of the world. But although this did not happen as visualised, it has remarkably proven to be the end of the world *as we have known it*. And it is worth noting that the Mayans themselves thought that the end of their Long Count Calendar would bring about a 'transformation'.

There is no doubt that there are now new finer, lighter, more powerful energies radiating onto the earth emanating from extraordinary sun activity that have now begun to impact the way we live our lives. There are the worrying effects of climate change and the speeding up of time, both of which are now matters of wide interest with people everywhere aware of global warming and remarking on how time is flying. And it is a time of considerable global unrest.

It was around the time predicted by the Mayans that there occurred what has since been called The Shift, when we became aware that these new frequencies are taking mankind from a Third Dimensional existence where Ego holds sway and we regard ourselves as being a separate entity from everyone else, into the peace of the Fifth Dimension when mankind will have realised the truth of his being, that we are all one in spirit and share a Collective Consciousness. In this context a Dimension is not a place but a state of consciousness and we are now on the Fourth Bridge of Transition where we are meeting all kinds of difficulties in our striving towards the Fifth.

Part of The Shift has been the effects of the rapid development of technology that enables us to know and see what is instantaneously happening elsewhere in the world. This open window onto the world is proving to be most unsettling. In addition to the educational benefits of seeing animals and nature in their own habitats, we are also able to witness for ourselves the pollution and poisoning of the land and oceans caused by human selfishness and thoughtlessness. And we cannot look at our televisions without being confronted by war, genocide and distressing acts of violence as they actually occur. Equally, it is heart-breaking to see millions of homeless refugees hopelessly living in tented camps in meagre conditions. These pictures imprint on our minds and are, I believe, beginning to play a part in bringing nations together for the benefit of all.

Understandably, there is a great deal of discontent throughout todays world and whole populations are saying "Enough" to exploitation, oppressive regimes and the inequalities that abound everywhere. The intolerance between religions is resulting in wholesale murder and savagery, in spite of the fact that all religions are founded on Love and Peace. But terrorists and extremists still held by Third Dimensional standards think that by spreading fear they can force others to adapt to their particular idolatry. They have no respect for the differences they find in others, but use those differences as a platform from which to launch enmity and hatred.

But in this Fourth Dimension, under the influence of the new vibrations and frequencies now streaming down upon us, we *will* begin to see that humanity is one Consciousness and recognise that we are all affected by what is happening on the other side of the world.

In our circle we found that we could invite our Higher Self to join our meditations and recognising the need to allow the new vibrations to permeate through us, we sought to bring balance into our lives by allowing thoughts from the Heart to expand. This meant subduing the Ego to deal with those things that have form and are essential to our physical existence, and allowing our guiding thoughts to come from the higher consciousness of the Heart. We recognised the need for control of our thoughts and subsequent actions, and of projecting kindness and patience to all with whom we came in contact. This is not at all easy when we are met by Third Dimensional negative attitudes and behaviour, but the Fourth Dimension is essentially a period of great trial and difficulties and we should not expect an easy ride. But let us remember that Light will always penetrate the darkness.

CHAPTER 22 - THE MIRACLE

It was in the autumn of 2013 that I had a complete collapse and found myself in Worcester hospital with leukaemia, seemingly unconscious to the world, yet, so I am told, sometimes talking to doctors and visitors without being aware or remembering a word. I do recall however, that it was agreed I should go into a hospice and the consultant said he would book a bed. I have very little recollection of the passing of days although I felt quite comfortable and resigned to my passing into the next world. I was then asked to have a bone marrow test. But a voice in my head kept repeating "You don't need it. You don't need it" over and over again. And so true to my guidance from spirit, I was adamant in my refusal and refused further treatment.

A few days later I was transferred to my small local hospital, although at that stage I had no strength and was still unable to walk or do anything for myself. A great deal of what happened was again blanked out, but I do recall some of the disruptive and irrational behaviour I displayed under the influence of morphine and other strong drugs. I vaguely remember refusing my medication from a mature nurse, being absolutely convinced that she had already given it to me. And on another occasion I told a patient she was in a bed that had the wrong name over it, and warned her to be careful or she might be given the wrong medication. I must have been a trial, or a great joke, I don't know which but I was put into isolation! I spent the next couple of weeks there during which time I had my 93rd birthday and held court with a large cake and many visitors came taking over the ward and the corridor outside. Blessedly I made a speedy recovery largely due to the wonderful young nurses who all wanted a copy of my book and took every opportunity they could to discuss it with me. They also took great interest in my collection of crystals and stones that I had with me. Eventually I was sent home with four carers and lots of other help, and I was determined to become independent again.

In the New Year I went to Worcester hospital for my final visit to the wonderful consultant who had looked after me so well.

He greeted my daughter, Jose', and myself with a big smile and leaning forward in his chair he said, "It's all gone."

Bewildered I asked, "What's all gone?"

And he repeated, "It's all gone. Your blood is perfect," and then added, "we don't know how it started and we don't know why it finished, but it's gone."

Then he continued again, "Could it have been Spiritual Healing?"

Looking at him in amazement, I ventured "How do you know about that? Did I talk to you about it?"

"Yes," he affirmed, "and I have read your book." He watched my face and then simply said, "It is a miracle."

My gratitude to him and those in Spirit who brought about the miracle and to those of my Group who came to both hospitals almost every day to administer healing, although I have only fragmented memory of their doing so, is boundless. And I bless my daughter and those other friends and neighbours who constantly brought me their Love and were there for me when I needed them so much.

Of course, I was compelled to ask myself, my Higher Self and my wonderful philosopher guide Ephriam, over and over again, "Why had this happened? Why did I survive? What am I meant to do?" Nevertheless it was not until three years later, after I had moved into the country some distance from the South Midlands and my life had completely changed, that I had the inspirational thought that I should rework my book "Many Doors". It had been written in 2000 and published the following year, and I now understood that it was incomplete and should be revised to include the work we did in the new circle and our understanding of the Shift from the Third into the Fourth Dimension. Importantly, it should also include the part we are being asked to play in the Collective Consciousness in this extraordinary transition into the New Age, and what is more, give guide lines on how this might be achieved.

The thought of revising and expanding my book was very appealing, and following the pattern of my life, there immediately occurred a synchronicity in the shape of a young man Matthew, who offered to get it published it for me. Blessings abound!

When I had left the South Midlands the Group moved to another town and continued their meetings under the guidance of a leader from within the Group itself. It is wonderful that I have been able to visit them twice a year to give a talk and renew our close bonds of Love and friendship.

In retrospect my years of dealing with lost souls, hauntings, psychometry and other psychic phenomena were most valuable in as much as they convinced me of the absolute reality of the ethereal world beyond the veil. They were really fantastic experiences that provided me with a solid foundation upon which to develop my connection with my Higher Self and Guides. Unfortunately, I have not had the opportunity of doing any psychic work since I moved into this rural setting, but blessedly, the healing I am privileged to channel through my Healing List and through ten other Healers, is as strong and effective as ever it was.

CHAPTER 23 - DEEPER UNDERSTANDING

Every week in the last Development Circle I would give a talk for discussion or meditation. The aim was to assist the sitters' spiritual development by introducing ways and means by which they could control their Chattering Mind and deal with the small irritations and annoyances of daily life. And there is no doubt that as most of our lessons come to us through interaction with other people the Group learned the necessity of tolerance, patience and respect. Basic to everything was control of the Ego with the added premise that what we think today we become tomorrow. The meditations during which we met our Higher Self, our Guides and other High Beings, were highly valued and our visions and communications were openly discussed for the benefit of all.

I also introduced the Watcher, who is actually an aspect of our connection to our Higher Self and is always on hand to guide us through our Heart Thoughts. We accepted that we have been born at this time with the express purpose of assisting in this unique transformation of mankind, and the Watcher is part of our inspiration when we have choices to make. We also found that our ability to direct Light, Love and Compassion not only to individuals but also to peoples in the dark places in the world, changed our perspective not only of humanity, but also of ourselves.

Consequently, a selection of those talks have been edited and are to be found in the second half of this book along with practical meditations. Hopefully they will encourage readers to investigate for themselves their reason for being here at this particularly turbulent time. It will take courage to view the turmoil in the world without some trepidation, but ahead lie innumerable possibilities and choices, and if we can keep our faith and use our Freewill wisely we will open doors to the new home of a new mankind …. Homo Spiritus in the 5ᵗʰ Dimension.

TALKS TO THE GROUP

SELFLESS SERVICE
2010

For several years our spiritual development and healing group has been receiving guidance and tuition from the spirit world and we have become acutely aware of their presence among us. There are Guides we can recognise and communicate with, but others who influence us are still unknown to us and may never be known. The purpose of this close interaction is to make us aware of who we truly are, why we are here on this Earth plane and to lead us to our highest good.

We have examined the philosophies of many spiritual teachers, but however much we may read books or articles or however much we listen to fine speakers, we are only able to accept their doctrines according to our current level of inward understanding.

We will know that we have developed deeper spiritual insight when we feel differently about the world around us and our perception of our fellow men has undergone a profound change.

A huge step forward will be when we can, without any reservation, regard all men as part of the Brotherhood of Man, issuing from the same Source and Energy as ourselves. Their circumstances may be entirely different from our own, but recognition that they are also on the spiritual pathway back to the Source (or God) via the many realms in the spirit world, opens us to a compassionate view of the world and all its peoples.

Our ultimate aim is to feel Unconditional Love for the whole of humanity and nature, even including those people who irritate us, deceive us or wish us ill. This is aiming very high and may not be achievable in this lifetime, but it is an aim well worth working for. Even the effort in this life time will be inspirational and contribute to the development of our own spiritual progression and at the same time, contribute to the state of the world as a whole.

We understand that the guidance and inspiration sent to us comes from the highest it is possible for us to receive – even far beyond our own known Guides. And it should never be forgotten that man has been blessed with Free Will with which to make choices about how he decides to live his life.

And in making choices we must always remember that the support we receive from the Spirit world is meant to inspire, guard and guide us, it is never intended to be followed slavishly and run our lives for us.

As we progress with new awareness and understanding, we will find that our Gifts of the Spirit will begin to naturally unfold and develop. The result may be the ability to channel messages from those who have passed into the higher life, or channel the healing energy as a healer, or convey spiritual teachings etc. All of you will become conscious of the truth of everlasting life. These gifts of the spirit are channelled to and through us for the benefit of mankind, and we should develop them and use them in service to others without thought for self.

SPIRITUAL HEALING
2010

Sickness and ill-health are not punishments imposed by God, but are the result of breaking natural laws that govern our world. The law of Cause and Effect cannot be avoided and a good deal of ill-health is due to ignorance and originates in the mistreatment of our causal body including wrong diet, poor relationships, wrong thinking, and the stresses of modern life.

Spiritual Healing is often called Faith Healing by those who know little about it, and Faith can indeed play a large part in what takes place. But some remarkable cures have occurred with animals, children and others too weak or ill to know what is going on.

Healers are instruments of those on the other side of life, usually doctors who were highly skilled on earth and who, motivated by Love and the desire to progress spiritually, now wish to serve mankind. Healers too, should be motivated by Love for mankind getting as near to Unconditional Love as it is possible for them to get. They should have complete Faith in the healing process believing that they can bring wholeness and perfect health to their patients.

The method used may be the laying on of hands backed by prayer to the Great Spirit or Source for Spirit guidance, and is carried out as simply as possible following the inspiration and guidance of the Spirit Healers. Or possibly the Healer prefers a method where he does not touch the patient and works through the field of psychic energy that constitutes the aura, but either way he should always open the healing session in prayer for Spirit Guidance. A Healer will come to know which method gives him the best results.

144

When commencing healing it is desirable that the patient is sitting comfortably and then taken into state of complete relaxation and well being. This may be induced by gentle stroking of the forehead and moving the hands sideways out of the head's aura. Care must be taken NOT to draw the internal blood circulation from the forehead over the head to the nape of the neck as this may cause fainting. Healing should always end with brisk, light circular movements of the hand DOWN the spine three or four times to invigorate the patient.

The end result is often influenced or determined by the patient's mind-set. He may have come to the Healer as a last resort when it may be too late for anything to be done, or old age may mean it is too late for regeneration. There are cases where a patient may have an unconscious desire not to get better because of his need to be the centre of attraction. Or it may be that he has completely accepted his condition and cannot imagine life being anything other than it is. He may of course, just wish to die. But apart from these unusual situations, there is always some betterment and remarkable relief and cures do result.

When a Healer attends a person who is on the verge of passing into the next world, he can induce a state of complete calmness and peace just by holding the patient's hands and silently praying for a peaceful and guided passing.

Absent Healing is most effective when undertaken at a regular time each day or week, and, I repeat, the session should always open in prayer. Patients given Absent Healing may not be aware of the Healing and Love directed towards them, but good or remarkable results can ensue. Whatever method used, no Healer can or should guarantee a cure. He can only open himself to be a pure channel for the Divine Healing Energy and do his work with humbleness of heart.

Spiritual Healers should never pretend to be doctors or have medical knowledge. And they should not have preconceived ideas about diagnosis, but leave that to spiritual guidance from their spirit counterparts. They should observe personal hygiene, always wearing clean clothes and ensuring they have no signs of stale sweat or bad breath. They should always be cheerful and encouraging to induce in the patient a state of positive optimism, encouraging him to expect betterment or wholeness without promising a cure. It is helpful to encourage the patient to undertake repeat visits so that improvement may continue to build up.

Healers should ensure that patients follow their doctor's advice. If a Healer thinks that medication is producing bad side-effects he should advise the patient to see his doctor again – he should never countermand a doctor's advice or stop prescribed medicine.

A Healer should never treat a person who has mental illness, except with the agreement of the doctor which should be sought in writing by the Healer. They should never treat pregnant women. A male Healer should never attend to a woman without the presence of another person within call. Children up to the age of 16 must have an adult in attendance or in the next room.

Healers should keep accurate, detailed records of each patient and ensure that they are covered by a Therapists' Insurance to deal with potential charges of malpractice and errors and omissions.

THE LIFE FORCE
2011

We are all aware that television and radio waves are accessible to us because we have found out how to tap into their individual frequencies. By pushing buttons we can use their invisible wavelengths to hear sounds and see pictures for our amusement. Furthermore, there are many other aspects of modern technology in which we use other invisible frequencies such as X-rays, ultra sound, micro-waves etc to improve our health and quality of life. That we can use these technologies is proof that although they may be invisible to the eye, they do actually exist and are actually controllable.

In the physical world everything we can see, everything we can touch and everything we can hear has its own vibration. We use one of our five senses to translate a particular vibration into something we can see, touch or hear. The vibrations of music give us tunes and the vibrations of voices give us songs. Some vibrations give us colour whilst others give us form, because everything that exists is resonating. All the things that are visible to us and all things we can touch and feel are vibrating to a particular frequency. As an illustration – because a chair vibrates at a specific frequency we can see it as a chair, but if it vibrated at a different frequency we would see it as something quite different.

Beyond the narrow waveband of the physical world, there are other wavebands where vibrations are of lower or higher frequencies. Among the lower frequencies are heat waves, short and long radio waves and micro waves. The higher frequencies include gamma-rays, X-rays, ultra violet and doubtless other unknown frequencies waiting to be discovered.

The Astral Plane to which all human beings transcend after their lives on earth, is a wide band of vibrations higher than those we now know and use in the physical world, some parts of which can be perceived by psychics and sensitives. This spiritual world is also part of Cosmic Energy that is within everything seen and unseen, known and unknown.

We are now aware that Quantum Science has proved that Cosmic Energy cannot be created neither can it be destroyed. To change form in the physical world, that is, to change from one thing to another, it is necessary for there to be a change in vibration. An illustration may be the cycle of clouds, rain, rivers, oceans and clouds that involve water droplets, and steam, mist, vapour etc. These are all manifestations of water in various forms and changes in energy vibration may also produce fierce weather in which water occurs as tornados, thunderstorms, hurricanes, cyclones etc. But the total amount of Cosmic Energy is constant, it cannot be added to nor can it be decreased or destroyed.

As Human Beings are part of both the physical and spirit worlds we, in common with everything else in the Universe, are made up of energies that cannot be destroyed. Thus, at the change we call death it is our invisible Etheric body that carries the human spirit into its next phase of existence. In the Afterlife the Spirit is a continuum of the same Life Force – the same spiritual essence that energised the physical body. It has not died, but it has changed to a higher vibration in order to adapt to its new life in the Astral plane.

THE CHATTERING MIND
2011

Some little time ago we discussed the power of the Chattering Mind that intrudes upon our thoughts and what we may be doing at the time, dragging us back into the past often inducing guilt and regret about something we may once have said or done. But as we know, it is just as likely to randomly take us into the future in a state of 'what if' making us fearful and anxious about things most unlikely to ever happen. It is not often that people live in this precise moment – in the NOW – and experience what they are doing in full awareness. Their normal state is to be doing one thing whilst their thoughts are flitting from one thing to another quite unrelated to the present task. And actually, the chain of thought is itself interesting, and one wonders how it jumps from one subject to another – and sometimes what the connection might be, or if there is a connection at all.

But the Chattering Mind is actually the Ego talking to itself. Making itself aware of itself, and being happy with itself – which really is all it is interested in. It is always trying to promote and defend itself. It is at the root of selfishness and is determined to prove itself (that is you) right and others wrong, or at least blameworthy of your situation. The Ego sees itself as separate from everyone else, and we look out at the world as though we are at the centre of it.

It is the Ego who disrupts relationships by excessive pride and the propensity to look for slights and criticism where none exist. And the past is coloured by the Ego's view of events, so that it prevents you looking at yourself honestly and frankly, when you really need to be trying to understand where you went wrong and how you contributed to a particular situation. And you really do need to know to prevent making the same mistake again.

It is not until we are consciously focusing on some matter on hand that we can ignore the incessant chatter. We may be deep in a book, cooking, making something or the other with our hands, or concentrating on calculating figures, working our computer, knitting or something equally absorbing, it is then that we can be said to be truly living in the moment – that is, living in the Now untroubled by either the past or the future. You may know this type of concentration as Mindfulness.

However, there is another way of living in the NOW and that is through the happy, relaxed state of meditation. Meditation is an altered state of consciousness, in which we sit quietly with the deliberate intention of raising our vibrations above that of the Chattering Mind, and have entered a state of pure Being, melding with our Higher Self in perfect Peace. In this state our Ego is completely subjugated and has lost control of the physical person it would like us to think we are.

It is true to say that in this relaxed altered state of consciousness our experiences are of higher intensity. The colours and pictures we visualise are sharper, clearer and brighter than we normally see with our physical eyes. And after much practice and to a greater or lesser degree, you may become aware of the inside of your physical body and experience tingles and changes in the vibrations of the Chakras and organs within you.

I am sure you have found that if you can control the Chattering Mind it is not difficult to feel the presence of you Guides and mentors. You may not know their names, which is not important. You may occasionally see them, but not all the time. But you should be aware of their presence and be able to recognise individual Guides by the particular feeling or sensation they bring to you. You will also become more sensitive to the intuitive thoughts being sent to you, and be more able to recognise and trust your intuition knowing it to be spirit guidance.

There is no doubt that your journey through this life must involve unselfishness and service to others and as you progress you will naturally find yourself helping others in many different ways. However, you came into this life to learn certain lessons for your own spiritual progression, a task that must not be neglected. Part of your progress will depend on the extent to which you can increase your tolerance of others and curb what you might regard as natural judgement of them. This means that you will find that you can ignore the influence of the Ego's desire to put yourself first, and that it will become easier for you to do this as you become more attuned to your Higher Self.

And so gradually, as your aura changes and reflects your progression, you will send out new vibrations to be picked up by others who will be attracted by the qualities of kindness, love and compassion they sense in you. And although you may not know it, you will become be a source of inspiration and unconsciously open doors for them.

And if we continue to live in a state of Gratitude for all the small things in our lives that up to now we have taken for granted, we will live in a state of Trust, knowing that we are truly Blessed and cared for by those closer to us than our hands and feet.

WHAT IS SPIRITUALITY?
2012

What is Spirituality? One would hope that we would always find spirituality at the heart of religion as religion involves a sacred Deity or God. But unfortunately that is not always the case. I think we all know people who regularly attend a church of some denomination or other who may regard themselves as spiritual because of their attendance, but from our point of view, they greatly miss the mark. This must mean that our notion of spirituality must be very different to theirs.

If we asked random people about their understanding of spirituality, they might have the idea that it must have something to do with spirits and what is called the supernatural. And if you use the word supernatural you would be assuming that there are spiritual beings but that they transcend what is natural – that is, they are unnatural to the general order. And what is more – if supernatural can mean that it is beyond being natural it can mean that it can possibly be untrue.

There are as many ideas about what is natural, and what is supernatural as there are religions. But religion and spirituality are not the same thing. We can experience either without the other – religion without spirituality and spirituality without religion. And you will recognise that here in this group we try to understand spirituality without the religion. So what are we really trying to achieve?

We now readily accept that we ourselves are spiritual beings living a physical life for the purpose of learning from our experiences. This is something that we may have been saying for years before we were able to feel it with deep conviction. True conviction comes when we feel connected to the inhabitants of our real Home in the Astral plane.
And of course I refer to feeling connected to the Guides and Guardian Angels who try to guard and guide us through this plane of existence.

The ability of our Guides to guide us, and our Guardian Angels to guard us, depends to large extent on our spiritual understanding and our willingness to be led. The small voice of our own conscience will often tell us right from wrong, but in hindsight something we thought was right may often turn out to have poor consequences because we have not been guided by our Higher Self but by our Ego.

The Ego was given to humans for self preservation, to protect them from other humans and the natural dangers of the natural world. His Ego has also helped man to evolve through giving him a sense of pride and belief in his own abilities. Thus man has been able to explore the earth on which he lives and protect and defend his family, his home, and the things he considers to be valuable and necessary to his existence .... even to the extent of going to war and killing other humans if he feels, or is told, that something precious is being taken away from him. But the Ego can do more than defend, it can also be aggressive if it is thought that some other faction of society has something that should rightly be his.

Let us understand that irrespective of where we live, mans' own Freewill has always determined the type of society we create. Throughout history mankind has proved to be cruel and oppressive, firstly tribe against tribe and then country against country until during the horror of two world wars there were various alliances, culminating in mass destruction in wide areas of conflict. All this, in what we call a civilised world. And when the Ego completely takes over it can create a megalomaniac mind such as an Adolf Hitler.

So what then is Spirituality? I think I would call it insight into the values of the higher realms of being and the higher aspects of Love and aspiring to live to our highest potential. As we move towards the 5th Dimension we begin to understand that our task is to balance our spiritual understanding with the force of our Ego. This means taking pleasure in giving and sending out love to others, recognising that they too are spirits on a pathway of evolvement and transformation.

We should not be looking for slights or misunderstandings, or be critical of the actions of others which may well be the best that they can do according to their understanding. We must find it in our hearts to overlook or ignore the hurtful remark or the let-downs that would have upset us, or made us angry, in the past. And as we grow and become more enlightened it will become easier and easier to accept people as they are without criticism. And as you can imagine, when we are able to reach this stage, we will feel so much happier in ourselves.

It is worth reminding ourselves here, that when we allow other people to upset us through their careless words or actions, our Ego will see that as giving them power over us. But when we are in balance our spirituality will tell us that they need our compassion and understanding.

Now, in this small group, and many others like it, we have become aware that we are involved in the gradual process of transition into our High Self. We are trying to allow the influence and wisdom of the Higher Self to guide our thoughts and actions. And we can truly be said to be on the pathway to enlightenment by learning to communicate with those who live in another dimension and have our highest interests at heart.

It is now that we are being gently inspired to help others to know the truth of their being by "opening doors" for them. This is a natural part of our own progression and requires a measure of sensitivity. It is not easy to recognise where there is the opportunity to say the right word or lend the right book to the right person at the right time.

At this stage of your understanding you will not feel rebuffed or take offence if it appears to come to nothing, because your friend has the Freewill to say "No thank you", but on the other hand, as so often happens, you may have sown a seed that will blossom just when it is needed.

What we are trying to achieve is more than words. Words are meaningless until we bring their understanding into practice in our daily lives. We need to watch ourselves and practice giving love and sending out love until it becomes a natural way of living.

Believe me – you will know when you are allowing your heart and Higher Self to rule. You will experience a new joy in living, a sense of wellbeing and lightness of step, peace in your heart and gratitude for everything around you.

WHO YOU ARE
2012

I told you last week that we had experienced death before we came into this incarnation – and you seemed surprised! And I was surprised that you were surprised. I would like to expand on this because it is important that you recognise who you really are. Not just in words but also in terms of feeling and being who you really are. And to recognise that for better or worse, your belief system creates your reality and your state of health.

The release of knowledge on the planet is growing very fast. Incredibly it is as recent as in my lifetime, but not in yours, that Albert Einstein a German Jew, discovered that everything we can think of including Planet Earth and the Universe are made up from Cosmic Energy. And he asserted that the various frequencies of that energy's vibrations determine whether they are visible to us in some kind of form, or are so high that they are invisible. And across the planet more and more people are recognising that we are more than a body who happens to have a spirit but that we are actually a spirit who has a body made up of the elements of the earth.

The dictionary says that death is being without life, but acceptance that death is a transition from one level of consciousness to another of finer vibration – has to be an early stage in your understanding and development. You will also come to the realisation that we have experienced life and death many times during our eternal life, and will continues to do so, not only here, but also through the various planes of spiritual existence.

I realise that early stages of our development are not easy as they involve trust and acceptance of spiritual concepts we may not have previously heard of. We are asked to accept our Spirit Guides as a reality even before we can feel their presence or communicate with them. We are also asked to fully accept, without a shadow of doubt, that although we are solid physical human beings, there is within us not only intelligence through our physical brain (what we might call our intellect or cleverness), but that we are part

156

of a Higher Self that is the spiritual essence of who we really are and who is the source of our Higher Wisdom.

Of course, this is not normally what we have been taught as children and it is understandable that some have great difficulty in dismissing their mental image of God as a man sat upon a throne, even though they may think it is really ridiculous. And it can prove to be a real hindrance because visual images are hard to erase, and there is so much to unlearn. But when we get to know our Higher Self and can communicate with It, we will bring new insight and wisdom into our lives.

Before being born into the physical world we were aware of what we needed to learn in this lifetime and together with our Higher Self we laid the preparations. Can you imagine how very precise and complicated these preparations were? They involve many energies that combine and interact to provide you with the tools you will need to equip you for your mission here.

Your parentage, social circumstance and country were exactly chosen, and the era in which you are born is of course, important. Human nature being as aggressive as it is, it is quite likely that you may be born in time of war or be required to live in its aftermath. You may have a physical disability to overcome. We are all so individual, but we will all be confronted by the experiences we need and which we have drawn to us. I have often heard it said that life is unfair, but be assured that life is fair and irrespective of our status in society, from the highest to the lowest, we will all have our own trials and tribulations and our own experiences and lessons to cope with.

But the great blessing is that you have been given the gift of Freewill and you can choose how you walk your pathway. In fact your life will always be a matter of making choices, and subsequently living by the choices you have made. Furthermore, Cause and Effect play a large part in everyone's life and very often the choices you have made resulted in ill health because of lack of understanding of your true nature or perhaps through false ideology or wrong living.

Part of progression is to understand (and this may be difficult), that you bring events into your life through your own thoughts, choices and actions, and in spite of outside influences, you are now where you are because of choices you have made. And the reason this may be difficult and uncomfortable to hear and accept, is because we so often blame other people for our circumstances, or blame what we call "our nature" which may be the very thing we have come here to conquer.

But if we learn to meditate and communicate with our Higher Self and our Spirit Guides and act upon their guidance (which is always loving and gentle), we will become motivated by Love and Light, not only towards others but also towards ourselves. After all, it is by respecting our physical needs and spiritual selves in equal measure that we will bring balance, contentment, Love and good health into our lives. And they don't teach you that at school either.

Many believe that civilised man is fully developed but that is far from the case. The huge changes we are now experiencing will change us from Homo Sapiens to Homo Spiritus, a profound transformation that will bring about recognition of the Brotherhood of Man and Unconditional Love. The Fourth Dimension in which we are now living is a turbulent one, but you have all the inner strength and armour to bring you happiness and contentment in spite of what is going on elsewhere`.

.

What you probably have not realised is that your own spiritual progression is absorbed by the Higher Self and benefits Its own spiritual expansion. What you have learned and how you have applied that learning is also absorbed by the Collective Consciousness of humanity. It then becomes part of natural evolution, lifting and expanding the knowledge and direction of mankind for future generations. That is why you are so important – a drop of the divine in the ocean of life.

MAYAN CALENDAR
2012

We are now in November 2012 and well aware that the significant date of 21st December 2012 is rapidly approaching. It is the crucial date at the end of the Mayan Long Count Calendar that recorded the many cosmic cycles of the universe that in spite of their different lengths and diversity are forecast to all end at the same time. And the ancient Mayans did not reckon beyond that date.

There has been much speculation about the meaning of this coming together of so many different energies and cycles, and for some time we have become aware that new waves of energy are now coursing through our planet and changing not only mankind, but also everything else on it.

How can this be? Well, we know that everything is energy and the vibrations of an energy determines its form. We ourselves are spirits from another realm who are inhabiting the earth for what we call a lifetime, and have enrobed ourselves in a physical body made of the elements of the earth so that we may exist here. That we know and accept. If we cannot accept this concept of ourselves then we cannot hope to understand ourselves or the transition from the 3rd Dimension to the 5th Dimension that is taking place.

You who are here today are all experienced in meditation and aware of the nearness of our Guides and Guardian Angels, and there is no question that that they communicate with us to help and guide us through this lifetime. Each one of us has a Gift of the Spirit that may include clairvoyance, clairaudience, intuition, sometimes dreams, or perhaps spontaneous flashes of insight. Our linking with the realms of spirit is very close and I regard the dimension in which we live and the Astral Plane almost as one. And our connection is Universal Love that binds everything together in spirit.

When you hear this you quickly recognise that the 4th Dimension in which we now live is far from perfect. It is a material world that consists of anything that has form – that is length, breadth, height and time. There are also many energies in our Dimension that do not have form because they are emotions. Many are benevolent, compassionate, kindly and generous but others may be expressed as envy, revenge, materialism, lust, arrogance and selfishness. These emotions are the result of thoughts generated by our Ego, and this lifetime will give us the opportunities to deal with them wherever they are found.

The new energy that is now operating in various parts of the earth is a realignment of the frequencies that are within everything. After 2012 a new reality of consciousness will take over and humanity and the Astral Planes. It has been called The Ascension, the Resurrection and the Shift.

You may remember, the Resurrection was foretold by Jesus who is purported to have said "In the twinkling of an eye, the dead shall be raised and we shall be changed. But first" he said " the dead shall rise and then we shall be caught up together with them in the clouds" (i.e. the higher realms).

Our new understanding of this now, is that the Astral Plane will advance into a higher level of Consciousness and the Human race will advance into the dimension the Astral has vacated – so that we will in fact, advance together. And this will happen in the twinkling of an eye – that is, a relatively short period of time.

Humanity, Homo Sapiens as we are now, will naturally evolve into Homo Spiritus – that is a race with higher spiritual understanding and values than now. We will be living in a new, finer and higher dimension of Love that will include altruism and a consciousness of the oneness and inter-dependency of everything with everything else. This will come about when humanity can handle it – it will be on a heart-centred wave band or frequency of consciousness, sending out Love and Light to the whole world. And when enough people are living at that level the second Shift into the 5th Dimension can and will take place.

It will not actually take a great many people to create the tipping point because the higher Consciousness is powerful and responds to prayer, Love and the Collective Consciousness of mankind.

We are being told that it will be the most glorious transformation in recorded history. And as a higher Love takes over the world, Peace will descend and war will be in the distant past. If this sounds improbable, or even impossible, remember that our race of men evolved from apes and at one time practised cannibalism. Even just a few centuries ago, we practised other tortures such as public hanging and quartering that we now regard as disgusting and totally unacceptable. And slavery was endemic until very recent in our history. But even so we have a long way to go as modern warfare has now become more vicious involving civilian populations and massive destruction of property.

What is happening and has always been happening, is the natural evolvement of the human race but this particular transition is like nothing we have experienced in recorded history. Nevertheless, those who believe that the change will be a wonderful transformation and are willing to take part in it without fear, will easily make the journey.

So what are we required to do? Obviously we need to be fully aware through all our senses and heart thoughts, who we really are. We need to control the negative emotions of our Ego and our attitudes towards others. We must acknowledge our continual need to evolve towards enlightenment and we will do this by following our inner guidance, intuition and our Heart thoughts. And the lives we live will reflect our progression.

WORKING WITH THE LI GHT
2012

For quite a long time now we have been meditating during which we have met our Higher Self and merged with the Higher Self, and in the course of which we have also met with Higher Beings who have added their love and energy to strengthen our connection to our Higher Self.

You are aware that the Higher Self and the Higher Beings are of a finer and quicker frequency than our human physical self. We may have visualised them as vague outline of beings, shadowy figures or bubbles of light, but now we are going to get a better understanding of who they are and what they do. And as our motives are purely for our betterment we will become closer to our Higher Self and the community of spirits to which the Higher Self belongs.

This community works with the Universal Mind and the Higher Will to bring higher energies to all those on the earth plane who are seeking their help or who are asking for assistance. Every call for help, every question we ask, is heard and acted upon. There is no criticism of what you may ask, there is only gentleness and a focus on the work at hand. There is humility too, because they are working solely for our progression with no thought for self – a fine example of the extent of unconditional love.

You are aware that they connect to us telepathically and part of your task is to expand your sensitivity to become more perceptive to their guidance. When you are in communication and there is something you wish to know, be clear what it is you wish to ask and frame your questions so that you receive more than a 'Yes' or 'No' answer.

You could for instance, ask to see your own personal Guides if they are not already visible to you. If you imagine that you are connecting, then you can connect. If you are doing some special project and ask for extra guidance, you will receive it. Just as you visualise yourself sending Light out to others, create in your mind Light being sent to you and you receiving it. Picture it coming into your own cocoon of Light, or directly into your Heart Chakra. Know that in receiving the Light you are allowing wisdom and insight to come to you, and understand that you can send the Light out to others without diminishing yourself, as the supply is endless.

As you try to live as your Higher Self – that is by making the right choices through right thinking, guidance and revelations will come from within rather than from without. That is because the Higher Self works on the subtle consciousness within your Heart Mind. So I would again urge you to be the Watcher and pay attention to your Heart Thoughts, your inner senses and your picturing.

And as you know, meditation is the powerful tool we use to become aware of the Higher Self and the higher elements. It is then that we connect through pictures, images, words and symbols and it is our interpretation of what is being channelled that defines what we understand to be the reality of what is being sent.

The more we become one with our Higher Self the more we will be connected to the soul consciousness of humanity and to all life-forms. We will appreciate the wonders of nature more, and understand our inter-dependence with all other forms of life. And as we perceive a closeness with other all life forms, we will inevitably experience sadness and concern for the way mankind has taken the whole of nature for granted and has desecrated everything for his own selfish ends.

So how can you help the living planet? Well you know that you can send out Light to wherever it is needed in the world. You can do this by sending messages of Love and Peace from your Higher Self to the Higher Self of others. You can also send out a gridwork of very fine Light and the images of Love and Peace will travel along this grid work to the person or place you have in mind. Let us try that ….

Just relax now, close your eyes, breath evenly and visualise a golden rod extending from 20 cm above your head, down your spine and under your feet for a depth of 20 cm. Still breathing steadily wait for your Higher Self to come to you and merge with you. Feel its warmth and Love. Think of a person now, a person close to you that you would like to send Light to. Imagine a fine golden grid-work of Light extending straight up from your crown chakra. Then imagine a line of Light from your Heart chakra to that person's Heart chakra. Visualise that person and mentally tell him or her that you love them as they are, not when they have changed their ways as you would wish – such as to stop nagging, or stop drinking or stop being awkward. Send them Love, Light and healing thoughts for whatever they need at this time, and sincerely Bless them. This will need to be repeated many times during the coming days and weeks, but you will be amazed at the results as the other person involuntarily reacts to the Blessing.

Bear in mind that there are great planetary changes under way and people have no option but to change with it and it follows that if you try and find stability in the outer world you may be confused and uncertain. But you can trust your inner guidance and wisdom. So go within and connect with your Higher Self and the higher dimensions, and you will find the stability and contentment we are all aiming for.

WATCHING THE EGO
2013

The talk this afternoon is about the Ego – that part of yourself that defines who you think you are. It plays a very large part in all your relationships and is responsible for the type of person you project to the world. You probably know it best for constantly reminding you of your past and dragging you back into various scenarios of "what if" you had done something differently, so that you may spend a lot of energy regretting and surmising. It can also make you fearful of something in the future and prevents you from living fully today when you should be living in Mindfulness and enjoying the present moment - the Now.

But perhaps you know it best as the "Chattering Mind". The chattering that, if you let it, would take over your meditation because it always wants to be in control. And for this reason alone you need to learn to quieten and subjugate the Ego. But to get a rounded view of the part it plays in your life, let me say at the outset that the Ego is a powerful motivating force in your earthly existence, one that you cannot do without.

It is responsible for your mind-set and gives you the encouragement to be successful in whatever you do. It is a driving force that motivates you to do things you can be good at, and it inflates your pride when you do well. This sense of pride in your achievements is a driving force towards perfectionism, or doing something better and better, such as in sports when long and arduous training and effort is essential. Or really in any activity where training, learning and practice is essential.

It is unfortunate that your successes in any field, and the satisfaction and sense of achievement they give, feed the Ego and make it stronger. It is the case that a person may be regarded by others as being strong, confident, self-motivated, powerful or a natural leader, because of the projection from their Ego. I would call that a positive trait but an excess of pride can result in too much self-satisfaction and ultimately arrogance, which, of course, should be avoided at all costs.

But it is how we see ourselves that is most important because we are often illusional about how we project to others. Robbie Burns was right – we don't see ourselves as others see us. It will only be when we are able to see ourselves clearly that we will recognise weaknesses and flaws within our make-up that originate in our Ego and are fed and fostered by the Ego. But this will always be a difficult issue, although at some time, if you want to progress, it will be necessary for you to face up to your own shortcomings.

So what sort of things in ourselves should we be looking for? Well first of all there is the conviction of being superior, or perhaps judging others and then feeling superior by contrast. And that judgment may include prejudice formed through adherence to a particular religion or political party. Or we may have had a head start in life by being fortunate enough to have been born into a privileged home with well-to-do parents, or perhaps had a better education than most. It is when we are successful in some area of our lives that the Ego can lead us into being dismissive of others who may have tried a lot harder than ourselves, but not achieved as much due to a lack of natural talent or being born into difficult circumstances.
However, we do have our Freewill and that gives us the opportunity of dealing with our circumstances in our own personal way. But we rarely recognise the influence of the Ego on our Freewill and that its intent to make us feel good about ourselves, is not always a good thing.

It is the Ego that is at the root of many of our reactions in dealing with others and causes so many problems in our lives. It may make us feel slighted when we are contradicted or being put in the wrong. It may make us feel we are being accused or attacked, even when we are not, and we may defend ourselves by becoming indignant and angry about nothing – the basis of many misunderstandings. The Ego will also provide us with all sorts of excuses rather than allow us to do something we fear. And an idle person can always find many reasons why they can't do something, because of the Ego's defence. From this you will see that the Ego does not judge between right and wrong, except that it is biased in your favour.

166

You probably know people who can always excuse their actions by believing in bad luck, or that the world is against them. They may have been born into an underprivileged environment where envy, prejudice and feelings of injustice and discontent are the norm. Their Ego's reaction is to make them feel hard done by and sorry for themselves that may eventually lead to bitterness and resentment. It is not surprising that such an outlook creates an inward imbalance and may trigger depression or some other debilitating illness, or even many illnesses, in the same person.

But when we start to think about subjugating the Ego let us be very careful not to throw the baby out with the bath water. Imagine life without the Ego. We could soon lose self-esteem and become somebody's doormat. Our get-up-and-go would soon become it-got-up-and-went. What would happen to ambition and belief in oneself?
How would we attain our goals? And what do we become if we don't take pride in ourselves and how we live?

We have to live in this material world and our Ego is an essential part of who we are. If it motivates us to do something well, or achieve a particular goal and we take pride in what we have done, it gives us a sense of wellbeing and happiness. We know it has been time well spent and we feel good about ourselves and we cannot feel good about ourselves and be stressed or fearful at the same time.

Surely the answer is to achieve balance in our lives – the balance between the Ego that is the physical and the spiritual that we are trying to develop. Let us be pleased with ourselves, approve of ourselves and love ourselves, but let us be watchful of where the Ego might lead us. But who or what will be doing the watching? What is it that will be nudging you to correct your thoughts or behaviour? Who or what will be assisting you along your spiritual pathway? Who is the Watcher?

There are many levels of consciousness on this earth plane and in the Universe that we are unaware of. And we ourselves function on many different levels of consciousness, some of which we are presently unaware. But just as the Ego is part of our consciousness, so is our Higher Self part of our consciousness. Both are part of our Total Self. The Higher Self is an aspect of us even though it is beyond the veil and it is also evolving spiritually as separate entity. Beyond that, it needs to be understood that the Higher Self will do all it can to assist our spiritual progress because our spiritual understanding, resulting from the experiences of this life-time, will add to the fulfilment and progression of the Higher Self itself.

It is when we decide that we have to deal with the failings within ourselves that we access a new level of consciousness that is the Watcher, a consciousness that is manifested by the Higher Self to help us. But even though the Watcher may identify a weakness the Ego will undoubtedly resent the correction and may be telling you to compromise, or even trying to convince you that you were right all the time.

But in your heart of hearts you will know what is right, and you will not be able to move forward until you can accept that you have this particular shortcoming to deal with. Then you must commit yourself to changing your perception of whatever it is that needs improvement or eradication.

So the closer you can align yourself to your Higher Self and bring the wisdom of the Higher Self into your life, the more balanced, healthy and joyful you will be. Ultimately your aim should be to seek contentment more than happiness. Happiness is a peak that is intermittent and doesn't last, but contentment has a depth that is immeasurable.

GIVING IS RECEIVING
2013

Everyone is yearning for Love. No matter our background, our upbringing or life experience, we all seek the approval of others. We want to be liked, we want to be approved of and we want to be loved. But we don't know what Love is – in its deepest sense we do not know what Love is. We know parental Love, sexual Love, family Love, friendship and Instinctive Love. Furthermore there is also Spiritual Love that cannot easily be defined as it has so many stages of development including Altruistic Love and finally Unconditional Love.

In the Ego's world we give gratitude, which is a part of love, when we have been given something we want, but our thoughts and actions may be very different if we have been disappointed in what we have been given.

If we seek true love through sexual love, or through our family and friends we will not find it. True Love will only come from self-knowledge and giving Love to all the people in our life. We need to give wholeheartedly, without reservation and expecting nothing in return – even when our gifts are not acknowledged and there are no thanks.

True Love cannot be earned and sometimes it is difficult to give, and what we normally call Love in relationships never satisfies our deepest longings. Because we have illusions about Love we have disappointments, suffer rejection and pain and even believe that Love can turn to hate. Which of course it never can if it is True Love and not infatuation or love reliant on our relationship with another person.

Part of our deeper understanding is to recognise that Love is not the outcome of an event or experience, it is a state of Being. We can only Be Love and know Love when we give it. Love means complete forgiveness not only of others but going deep within ourselves and forgiving ourselves for whatever errors or mistakes we may have made in the past. We do not need guilt in our life and this is one of the ways in which we ensure that the Ego loosens its grip on our thoughts. It is also essential that we see our past as experiences upon which to build our understanding of ourselves as we were at that time and as we are now.

The truth is that anything of real worth in this world cannot be bought and can only be increased by being shared. Just think about it for a moment, the emotions of empathy, compassion, forgiveness, understanding, acceptance of others and Love, are all unseen but have value beyond our awareness.

When we send out Love and Healing energies we have no idea how far they spread, because they are vibrations that reverberate far beyond anything we can imagine. This is why in our healing prayers we can ask for Peace in countries half way round the world knowing distance is not a problem – the ripples of our Love are never ending and eventually make their way back to us.

So the lesson is that our spiritual progression depends to a large extent, on our awareness of ourselves and to giving and not getting. When this is understood you will find yourself becoming a source of power for others. They will be able to draw strength through you, but not from you. The more you help, empower and strengthen others, the stronger spiritually you will become. In other words giving will be receiving.

But don't think that everything will then be OK because the Ego will not like it one little bit. It doesn't want you to give anything away. It always want you to put yourself first, so there may be difficulties, but the Ego will steadily lessen its hold and your duality of the physical and spiritual will come into balance and harmony – it just needs working on.

Finally, remember that it is the Watcher who will help you to be aware of your motives for all you say and do. And, please don't think that this is beyond you. There is an inexhaustible supply of Love in the world that is channelled to us to use in the highest possible way. And we can only BE Love when we give it. And in giving we will receive an expansion of higher consciousness that will take us into a constant state of sympathy and compassion for all others.

GROUP MEDITATION
2013

Last week we talked about getting the best from our meditations by undertaking exercises that enhance our five senses. It was not so long ago that people used to meet for meditation, relax quietly, and just see what they "could get". That was an end in itself. There was no expectation of connecting with spirit or receiving impressions. And I know for a fact that such meetings still exist and sitters benefit from the relaxation and come away with their batteries recharged and a heightened sense of wellbeing.

And you could do that here, but we want more from our meetings because we have a purpose. We are seeking spiritual progression, trying to raise our vibrations so that we may play our part in the transition into the 5th dimension.

Every meditation can be fruitful and rewarding when we can see clearly and hear clearly and understand what we are receiving. It is up to you not to be content with receiving something that is vague or not clearly defined that you do not understand. Colours need to be interpreted, shapes need to be formed into substantial pictures and symbols understood.

One of the objectives of your meditation is to get to know your Higher Self, merge with the Higher Self and obtain wisdom from the Higher Self. So do not be satisfied with hazy pictures, brief glimpses of pictures or people, colours that do not mean anything, or a vague feeling. These need to be developed and worked upon until you have a complete or much better understanding of what is being sent to you. This cannot be achieved overnight, although your progress to date has been wonderful, but it still requires a lot more work and perseverance. How quickly you progress will depend on the strength of your desire to succeed, the amount of time you are prepared to put in, and your faith and acceptance of what is happening.

So do not hesitate to let your Higher Self know if your meditation is unclear or hazy. Ask It to assist you in attaining closer communication. Be

172

careful not ask questions that require a Yes or No answer – that is not really helpful. Use what is known as open-ended questions in order to get a fuller reply in whatever way the answer comes to you.

This does not mean that your Higher Self is going to do the work for you. Your Higher Self will never take away your personal responsibility because it is part of your development.

But it is permissible for you to ask questions to help bring things into focus and widen your understanding. If you are seeing part of a face or picture, or if there is fragmentation of a picture or face, you could for instance, ask, "Can you bring that into focus for me a little more" or "What is it you are showing me?" or if you can't actually see someone, but can feel their presence, why not say "I can feel your presence. Could you come round the front and let me see you" or "I can feel your presence. What is you want or wish me to know?"

Part of your work will also be to interpret what is being sent and then remember what has occurred so that next time the same feeling or image arrives you will understand the language. This is particularly relevant when you are shown symbols, because you need to learn their meanings. They will become part of the language you will use when communicating. You will also come to realise that when you experience certain feelings, you can trust to associate those feelings to relate with certain conditions. I mean such things as feeling sad or happy, or being taken over by a feeling of apprehension. In such cases you ask … "I feel sad (or whatever) what does that mean?" and go on from there to develop the communication.

I will of course, always be pleased to help you to interpret what you have experienced, but eventually you will be able to identify what you are getting with greater clarity and trust. Perhaps you should always ask yourself – "What does this scene, feeling or symbol, mean to me?" and that will form a strong basis for interpretation.

You might find it comes easy to be aware of a person's name and even have ideas about whether it is a man or woman communicating. You might be

173

able to tell if a person is young or old and even get their exact age. These things might come as just a vague impression but I suggest that you accept them as being true. With practice you will be able to prove what is true and develop your faith that what you are getting is reliable and from your spirit communicator.

So you can see that when I go round the group and ask you to tell us what you have just experienced, it is helpful not only to yourself but also to the group. Everyone learns from everyone else's experience and bringing it out into the open helps to solidify your own experiences. It gives those experiences a reality and puts them into your sub-conscious to help you with similar repetitions in the future. So during mediation it is really helpful to everyone if you can remember what you have experienced and then put it into words for the benefit of all of us.

Meditations do vary and sometimes you will obviously be stronger or more relaxed than at other times, but that will be due to outside influences and whether you have been able to leave the world outside and have cleared your Chattering Mind when relaxing and opening your meditation. The Chattering Mind is of course, the Ego that does not want to let go of being in charge – not even for an hour or so. But it is important that you start your relaxation exercises by focussing on your breathing so that the Chattering Mind loses its power to interrupt, and you are able to meditate at a really deep level.

So to sum up – do try to meditate more than once a week even if you do not find it as powerful as being here where we share our power among all of us. And the more you meditate the easier you will find that you can attune to the higher vibrations of those beyond the veil.

LOVING YOURSELF
2013

Last week we spoke of the community of Higher Self Beings whose function it is to respond to the Higher Will for the benefit of the evolution of mankind. We learned how they connect to us telepathically and that part of your spiritual growth is to become more sensitive and intuitive to their guidance.

We heard how we can evolve to live as our Higher Self by making the right choices through right thinking and guidance that will come from within. This is because true guidance comes through your Heart Centre, your visualisation and your Heart Mind. And I reminded you to be the Watcher and pay attention to your thoughts, your inner senses and your power of visualisation..

This week we will look at the part that Self-Love plays in your development. First, it must be recognised that you are born with a unique temperament, one chosen before you were born. It is a core feeling within you and there is no-one else quite like you.

The type of person you could have been is endless. You may have chosen optimism, pessimism, happiness, resentment, melancholy, loneliness, seriousness or fun-loving. Some choose smugness or superiority whilst others feel unworthy and inferior, but whatever was chosen to be dominant in your persona, your birth circumstances have led you into experiences where these qualities may be expunged or developed.

I will be dealing with calming the emotions later, but for the time being I ask you to recognise that you are who you are to facilitate the experiences that are necessary for your progression. You have spent a very long time becoming aware that you need to love and forgive and tolerate others for whatever hurt they may have done to you. It has been an essential part of your spiritual progression, as has been the acceptance of people just as they are.

All that is difficult enough and when it involves certain people, it is not easily achievable. But what is most often overlooked is the need to love yourself. Not only forgiving other people, but also forgiving yourself. Not only accepting other people as they are, but also accepting yourself as you are, because every part of you - the negatives as well as the positives, are the essential you.

What I am saying is, learn to love yourself in your entirety. You cannot change your insecurities and negative feelings by hating them or denying you have them. Allow the Watcher to seek them out, and then you can change them by admitting them.
When you recognise that a negative thought has slipped through, the act of recognition is in itself a positive and you are on your way to eliminating the negative.

Remember also that negatives are part of your humanity – they are what you are here to experience and learn from. So love your negatives as well as your strengths for those are the areas that most need your love in order to progress.

Also remember to love your physical body and its functions. It is the vehicle by which you can live this incarnation. So bless yourself for everything little thing you are able to do – to cook, to eat, to walk and to drive. Bless your five senses and your heart for beating, your digestion for nourishing you and for your intelligence. Be aware of every part of yourself that makes you whole and additionally, use your time wisely.

There are Higher Beings in the spirit world continually sending Unconditional Love to all mankind, and we have been privileged to visit them in our meditations. You on your part are sending people your loving thoughts through the Light you are radiating when meditating or healing. Our Healing List is just one aspect of the Unconditional Love we channel when we allow ourselves to be instruments of those in Spirit who are devoted to healing those on the earth plane.

Don't forget that many of the people you meet with are younger, some much younger than you at soul level. They suffer from spiritual ignorance and aren't able to act kindly and lovingly so they are offhand and appear just uncaring. So learn not to react to others' rudeness, unkindness or perhaps lack of consideration. Don't let their thoughtlessness or even deliberate rudeness, hurt you even although your Ego may want you to retaliate in some regrettable way. Don't take offence if people don't treat you well. You don't know what has happened or is happening to them in their life, so do try to react with tolerance and even kindness.

It is wise to love and protect yourself by not allowing yourself to be drawn into another's unconscious pattern of thought. If you do let their behaviour hurt you and provoke you, you have given that person the power to lower your vibration even if only for a split second, when you know your true aim is to always keep it high so that your highest vibration can become your natural basic level.

There will be times when you will need to bite your tongue if you find yourself on the verge of gossiping and criticising someone – and I know it is not easy. We all do it because in village life in past ages, all people had to occupy themselves with was local gossip. So it is deeply ingrained in us to criticise and judge others so that we may feel above the crowd.

Loving yourself is about recognising the essential you and allowing yourself to be guided by your Higher Self. It means protecting your spiritual essence from anything that is vexatious because your reaction could have an adverse effect on your emotions and health. At the same time you will learn to Love and cherish those aspects of your Ego that keep you physically strong and positive in the material world.

In time, as you advance, you will naturally find yourself looking for the goodness in others, overlooking their imperfections and accepting them as they are. And the more you are able to look for the best in others the more you will come to find that the world around you is a more beautiful place in which you will find a deeper inner contentment than you can now possibly imagine.

HEART CONSCIOUSNESS
2014

I have entitled today's talk Heart Consciousness, but to arrive at the Heart Consciousness, I have to start once again with the Ego that for thousands of years has been our guiding principle.

The Ego's struggle to maintain and exercise control of our lives is in many respects actually destructive because it resents the challenge of spirituality that encourages us to be of service to others even if it is at a cost to ourselves. It is not unusual to find yourself questioning an unselfish answer to a problem because your Ego wishes you to put yourself first, even though in your Heart's thoughts you know that you could do better. If you listen to your Higher Self it will tell you that it is always better to be kinder and go the extra mile because everyone you meet has a private battle ground going on somewhere.

The evolvement of mankind's spiritual awareness has been a very slow process. But we have now arrived at a stage where millions of us throughout the world have broken away from formal religions and their control, realising that we can create our own pathway through the expansion of our state of Consciousness.

Let us look at what I mean by a state of Consciousness because all forms of life respond to specific conditions. Even mountains, the oceans, the winds and the core of the earth react to conditions that may or may not be predictable. We would not call that consciousness or even awareness, but it is a response because there is a cause and a natural effect.

Minerals and chemicals react to other chemicals in certain ways often depending on subtle and natural phenomena. Certain reactions are predictable which means that they can be controlled. But they are totally without consciousness and certainly without self-awareness.

It seems that the plant kingdom does have a form of consciousness although not self-awareness. They have unique patterns of reproduction and survival and respond well to the right nutrients and weather conditions. Conversely if they are subject to adverse conditions they fail miserably. And there have been interesting experiments where plants have responded to TLC and the human voice.

It is only when we look at the animal kingdom that we find a limited self-awareness that is predominantly due to the need for self-preservation. Some may be vegetarians but are themselves prey. But others prey on other animals and are aware that they are prey themselves. They experience fear and are highly instinctive, but are also capable of thinking and learning. Most animals and birds are protective of their young, some nurturing them much longer than others according to their species.

So everything we know to exist is governed by their particular instinctive consciousness and responds to certain stimuli in a predictable way. We are still learning how it all works and are aware that everything will be affected by the Great Transition that is now taking place.

But actually, my point is ... humans are the only living creatures with self-awareness of whom he thinks he is, thanks to his highly developed Ego. Where other forms of life follow their own limited instincts, man is unique in that he has within himself many states of emotion and consciousness. Through his Freewill he can choose to be a saint or sinner, kind or unkind, friendly or reserved, sympathetic or selfish, industrious or a slacker, a giver or a taker, a person who takes the rough with the smooth or one whose cup is always half empty. And he can be several of these, and much more, all at the same time in response to different people and different circumstances.

It is worth remembering that you also play many parts in life. At any one time you may be a husband or wife, a daughter or son, a father or mother, a friend or lover, an employer or a colleague, a grandparent or other family member, or you may even be a casual acquaintance. Wherever you are and whatever you are doing you will always be projecting a different facet of yourself depending on who you are with prompting the question .... Who are you really? And the answer is ….. a multidimensional creature, capable of existing at many levels of Consciousness all at the same time.

When you think about it, it is quite a feat to live as a human at all – we have so many diverse choices to make about how we live our lives. It can take half a lifetime before we even begin to think about who we really are - if we think about it at all. And when we do think about it the Ego gives answers that are acceptable to the five senses.

More often than not there has been a lot of disbelief and questioning before we have actually accepted that we are in essence a spirit who has chosen to live a very difficult life (incarnation) on this planet. Probably it was only when we became aware of our true spirituality that we began to look at how we live our lives.

It is very helpful at this point to recognise the value of involvement in some form of creativity – something in which we can take delight because it will be something that we have produced. It may be something very simple indeed that we might struggle to call artistic; such as growing something or designing something, or making something. I am thinking of woodworking, model making, knitting, painting or even baking a cake. It might turn out to be not very good, but you will have been exercising mindfulness, and using the alpha (artistic) side of the brain as opposed to the purely intellectual side.

It is up to us to see that we use both the alpha and beta rhythms in the left and right sides of the brain to bring them into balance and harmony. A balanced person can begin think with a Heart based consciousness that is the expression of spiritual values. This a huge step forward releases Ego domination of your thought processes and you will be making choices and decisions that are spiritually founded and wiser.

In your deepest consciousness, your soul does not want you to waste this incarnation and wishes to bring you to the highest level of consciousness you can achieve in this lifetime. It is your personal responsibility and entirely up to you as to the choices you make and the pathway you choose.

No-one can do it for you. But choose carefully, keep your eye on the ball, and listen to your intuition and the promptings of your Higher Self.

EMPOWERING OTHERS
2014

As you develop your spiritual progress, service and selflessness will become a meritorious natural part of your character. It is however, worth examining this more closely to avoid a serious misunderstanding. I would ask you to consider whether you might be a self-sacrificing person who gives far more than you receive? If so, you might be surprised to learn that it could be a big mistake. That mistake is to think that you are responsible for another persons' situation or understanding. It must be a mistake because everyone is personally responsible for their own happiness. And, when you think about it that is a blessing as everyone has the Freewill to create and change their own reality.

You can however, help someone to change their reality by empowering them which is quite different to just helping them. I am sure you are aware of the principle that if someone is hungry you can give them food, but they will be hungry again and seeking more help. And it is surely better that along with the food you also give them seeds so that later they may have the means to feed themselves.

Some people have chosen to play a very difficult role in this incarnation, and yet never seem to learn or progress. Or some rely too much on others to solve their problems for them. If you know someone like this who is over-relying on you, then it can be very difficult for you. But you can try and encourage them to be more self-reliant and independent. You are not here to "fix" other people, or stifle their initiative. They have to learn their own lessons in their own way and in their own time. It is your role to be supportive, perhaps tactfully suggesting ways to do or get something, or offering ideas of alternatives, whilst allowing them the freedom to make their own choices and choose their own pathway. There is no finer thing than to help another who is in difficulty or is inadequate in helping themselves.

Unfortunately, when you try and help people by empowering them, there is no guarantee that you will succeed for they may lack motivation or be afraid to take a first step. But the secret here is to know when they are ready to change and that isn't always easy. But it is helpful if at this time you put the problem to your Higher Self and listen to your intuition to receive the answer.

Heart based Consciousness is founded upon tolerance and acceptance of everything and everyone without criticism or judgement. Just BE and accept what IS. It is only when you truly understand that you are here to transform and heal yourself that things really start to change for you and for the people surrounding you, because of the Love you will be radiating.

The world is what it is at this particular stage of its transition, and the highest and noblest thing you can do is simply to love it for what it is and continue to send out the Golden Light and Love to everyone seen and unseen. You will be joining millions of others across the globe and beyond the veil who are working on the same vibrations of Love and Light, and you can play your part in the great transition by living your life to your highest good. In your healing and in your prayers or affirmations, you can ask that all mankind be guided to understanding spiritual realities, knowing that this will bring advancement towards the Brotherhood of Man and the ultimate peaceful unification of the human race.

SPIRITUAL GROWTH
2014

You will recall that I have recently spoken about the desirability of bringing balance into your life by engaging in some form of artistic activity. And I am mentioning it again, as it is so important to your long-term health and well being. I know we all have a lot to do, but we do need to find the time as it would bring the benefit of mindfulness and relaxation into your daily life.

But even without the introduction of a hobby I hope that you are leading a balanced life, and that you are not being held back by uncertainty, a sense of something missing, regret or guilt about something in the past, or fear – probably about something in the future. Or are you blessed with Love, joy, optimism and gratitude?

Knowing you, I would guess that you are probably neither all negative nor all positive, but have struck a balance that has made you satisfied with your life and made you happy. I would guess it is a state where you can focus on the NOW, and live every minute of every day to the full. It is a state of peace and contentment that we call the Presence or just Being, and comes from the Heart.

And now you are being asked to recognise that the definitive aim and reason for your incarnation is your own spiritual progression, although at first glance this might seem to be too much focus on the Self. But focussing on your spiritual progression cannot be regarded as selfish as your development must include helping others and empowering them to live their lives to their highest good. And it is well to understand that your motivation will come from your Heart Consciousness guided by your Higher Self.

The concept of having a Heart Consciousness might suggest different things to each one of us. What for instance do I mean by consciousness?

Do I mean awareness? Do I mean realisation? Do I mean enlightenment or insight? Do I mean seeing clearly – no that is clairvoyance! Words and meanings are difficult.

If we take Awareness, I am sure you will agree that lack of awareness is certainly a lack of consciousness and therefore also a lack of responsibility. Because if you are unaware -you are ignorant, and if you are ignorant you cannot be held responsible for what you do not know. And if you do not know, you aren't aware or conscious of what you not know.

But there was a time when you had an inkling that there was something for you to explore and that was the beginning of Awareness. This may have come to you through any number of ways, but it was a beginning and you may not even remember how it all began. But Awareness was not Consciousness – you were only reading the headlines not the substance.

But at the right time for you, you began to think that there is more to life than appears or something sparked your interest, and you became aware of the idea of having a spirit (not being a spirit but having a spirit) and you moved into Spiritual Awareness. Later you will have had a realisation that prompted you to seek further understanding. It was an open door. An invitation to explore more and satisfy your curiosity. You could have turned away, you could have taken a psychic pathway and ignored the spiritual. However, by taking the spiritual you will have found that you have opened your psychic abilities such as visualisation and intuitiveness that are a natural part of the many dimensions of Spiritual Consciousness.

We have now been given insight to the fact that most of our past thoughts and reactions came from the Ego, whom we had assumed was our identity. Under Its guidance we developed a deep sense of self-awareness that included being a special individual and being a big ME, often not accepting responsibility for our decisions, but blaming others for the situations we found ourselves in. We lived our lives protecting our Self.

And so you can see why we can often react to others instinctively and be prompted to retaliate to them thoughtlessly and selfishly – perhaps unintentionally hurting them in the process. Not very commendable but that is how civilisation works and how previous generations have lived their lives. And we too, try to stand out as a special individual in some way or another, often caring too much about what others may think of us.

You have all gone through gradual stages of understanding your true spiritual nature and your reasons for Being. And you are now in touch with your Higher Self, and with It's help and others in the Spirit world, you are able to channel healing energy and Love to those you know, and send out Love and Light to those unknown to you but need your help. Even so, your first duty is to your own spiritual progression, so what comes next? How can we progress?

Perhaps it would help to look at ourselves in a new light and grasp the perception that to have come this far, and gained this measure of enlightenment, we must be old souls who have reincarnated many times before. But in spite of all our many experiences, we still have to lot to learn and progression will not be handed to us on a plate – it is something difficult that we will have to work for in very challenging circumstances of the 4th Dimension.

To start with I suggest that you look at the people you judge, or criticise and find fault with, because what you dislike in them is often a mirror image of yourself - yes, they reflect the same imperfections within you that need attention and improvement.

I can give you some instances of what I mean. For example, you may think that someone is being obstinate, whereas if you act in the same way, you regard your own obstinacy as "being firm". Or, it may be clear to you that a certain person is interfering in a family relationship. But when you do the same you think of it as being "helpful". Another scenario might be that you think someone is "controlling", but you are doing similar things but justifying it as "caring". You may recognise when someone is being selfish or thoughtless, or perhaps you may accuse them of being uncommunicative, unreliable, gossiping, or tardy. You, yourself may be habitually inconsistent or unreliable but not recognise it in yourself, only

187

seeing it in others. Nonetheless, there are failings in others that you would not dream could possibly apply to yourself, but they are there.

I don't expect you to be happy to hear this because you obviously dislike what you are criticising and would hate to think that you could be accused of being the same. And so I know there are those who will have difficulty in accepting that this may be true. Yet, it IS true, and whether you accept it or not is in itself a useful pointer to your current state of growth. It is a fact that as you get to know yourself better and take responsibility for the corrections you need, you will find that the balance within you will have subtly changed and the Ego will have lost a lot of its power. It will have begun to confine itself to your physical vehicle and its strength and energy, whilst spiritual values will come more and more to the fore under the guidance of your developing Heart thoughts.

Unfortunately, personal pride that comes from the Ego can be expressed in quite unattractive ways, but I think that pride in ourselves might be the last thing we would want to lose. It is a great motivator and so essential in expressing ourselves to the outside world. We take pride in our appearance, our home, in our garden if we have one, our career achievements or winning a race. For some people pride it is their main driving force, but that could be quite objectionable when it borders on arrogance. So although we may wish to retain pride in our achievements and pride in ourselves, it is necessary to do so with a modicum of modesty.

Recognising small things that need to be improved will not be easy and really it will be endless, but the smallest correction is progress. And as subtle changes are taking place you will notice that you are less bothered by another's shortcomings or life style and more contented with just Being. You will be more in harmony with the flow of life even while acknowledging that there is more you need to know about yourself.

It is when you can accept people and the world as they are with tolerance and Love, and when you can Love and respect yourself just as you are now, that you can be sure that you are expanding your Heart Consciousness and allowing it to be your guiding principle.

188

REFLECTIONS
2014

On the last two occasions we met I spoke about Duality and our recognition of the two parts of our consciousness – the dominant physical Ego and the Spiritual side that is the spark of Divinity within us and is our true identity.

It is strange that we should have spent two weeks considering spiritual progression and how we should be trying to reduce the power of the Ego to allow the Higher Self to bring more inspiration and guidance into our lives. They were lessons that I should have taken notice of myself in view of an inward imbalance I was unconsciously creating and was totally unaware of.

You may remember that I had lost touch with my Guide, Ephriam (the philosopher), after I had asked that I should be guided for my highest good. When I saw him again in the courtyard in July last year with other High Beings, I asked him where he had been and he replied that he WAS the highest for me and pointed out that I had in fact, rejected his guidance. I recognised my mistake and ungratefulness and told him I was deeply sorry, and after that he has been waiting for me every week which was a big lesson and great joy to me.

I should say that at that particular time I was absolutely focused on my Spiritual work – researching, reading and writing to the exclusion of many other things I wanted to be able to do. Many times I said I would have liked to do some painting, but somehow I never got round to it. Holidays, theatre, listening to music, crocheting and knitting were all neglected too; but not, I hasten to add, my beautiful garden.

All might have been well as I felt happy and fulfilled, if I hadn't physically depleted myself in helping to take down large branches of my plum tree that had broken under the weight of its fruit. Although I felt fine whilst I was doing it, sometime during that night I completely collapsed.

You all know about my time in Worcester Hospital and the local hospital because several of you visited me, some many times, and gave me wonderful healing. It was a time when I thought I was going to pass on, and I was just 'being' without any coherent thinking.

But as you can see, it didn't happen and here I am. And I can never express my heartfelt thanks to you all and my gratefulness for your prayers. I cannot say that during all that time I was conscious of all the wonderful people who were praying for me and channelling healing to me. In both hospitals my underlying state was one of calmness and passivity accepting the fact that I was at the end of the road. Now of course, I am so grateful for all the Love that I know contributed to the miraculous spontaneous healing of my cancer and the rebalancing of my relevant charkas. I am so grateful too, to my daughter Jose' who ensured that I had daily visitors who brought so much Love and Healing when they came to see me.

As you know, we are a created consciousness who has chosen to come here for earthly experience. Nonetheless, I don't think any part of that earthly experience is meant to be anything like I went through. It was foolish of me to have created such an imbalance by neglecting my hobbies and social activities, so that I overloaded my physical body with high frequencies that were unsustainable. As an aged senior citizen I should have been watching my two friends slaving away at the plum tree, not assisting them.

But please do not think for one moment that you will create the same imbalance in yourselves – my experience will serve as your deterrent!

So I would say to you, ensure that you bring balance into your life by loving your whole self and do not deplete your body. Try your best to maintain equilibrium between loving your physical shell and your spiritual self. Do remember too, to be the Watcher and recognise any inequality without blame or guilt, simply because such recognition is progress in itself. Additionally, love your weaknesses as well as your strengths because those are the areas where it is necessary to make headway.

Finally, despite circumstances, try to maintain your sense of humour and find pleasure in everything you do. Moreover, be grateful for everything that comes your way, not because others are worse off, but because you feel gratitude for being you.

AMAZING GRACE
2017

There are many routes to long term spiritual development, and as you know, one of the most effective is meditation. Meditation in itself has many benefits, it quietens the mind, and stills your thoughts and emotions. You physically experience a calmness and withdrawal from everyday problems and worries, but true meditation has benefits beyond the physical. It provides space in which you can transcend to a higher level of awareness and it is possible to achieve clear insight of yourself as a balanced trinity of mind, body and spirit.

If during meditation we can achieve a state of Higher Consciousness in which we recognise the Unconditional Love that is showered on us by the Source, it releases in us an overwhelming sense of wellbeing and happiness. We can feel it swell our hearts with deep gratefulness - more than anything we have ever known.

In the past we have expressed Gratitude for something, and are aware that the Law of Gratitude, like the Law of Attraction, means that what you send out you will attract more of the same to you. Like always attracts like, and good will always attract more good. Furthermore, the power of Gratitude is particularly potent because to live in a state of Gratitude is to live in a state of Grace.

But let us look at how we might work towards a state of Grace – that is to know in your heart's core that you are Divinely loved and protected. Firstly it is desirable that your Gratitude be continuous and all encompassing. What I mean is, try and see the blessings in everything around so that your cup is always half full and never half empty and brighten your days by seeing the funny side of things.

It is your attitudes, your emotions and your understanding of natural Laws that attract success and happiness to you. You may think that you do count your blessings, but I wonder if you are grateful to your heart for beating so long and regularly, or your lungs for their rhythmic pulsations or your elimination and digestive systems for behaving so well? Bless them and they will respond healthily to your gratitude

I am sure you often think how blessed you are to live in a lovely part of the country and not in the slums of some big city. But have you ever thought how easily it could have been different had you not chosen the path that brought you there? Can you bring to mind the many blessings that have been yours and the people who throughout your life have been the "angels" who have helped to smooth your pathway? Have you recognised that they were the instruments of the Higher Realms sent to guide you along your pathway - and have you blessed them too?

You have so much to be grateful for that it is not difficult to make Gratitude part of your everyday way of thinking and Being. As your persona adjusts you will radiate Love and Compassion to the world and even on an "off day" you will be able to easily switch your thoughts to how blessed you really are, and any blip is just that ... a blip, nothing more. Everything passes. Life is one phase after another, but always be Mindful and Grateful and your life will become an amazing State of Grace.

FORGIVENESS
2017

When we send healing to those on our Healing List we are well aware that what we are sending is spiritual Love. It is not a maternal love nor a sexual love, but a part of Divine Love. It is the invisible aspect of the Light we can see with our psychic eye during meditation plus a heartfelt compassion. And because we are sincere in our intentions and are clear open channels, the Healing flows effortlessly and strongly.

Healing gives us the opportunity to practise Unconditional Love in its smallest beginnings without any bias or discrimination. We cannot change a person's behaviour. Only they can do that. But we can ask our Higher Self to communicate with the patient's Higher Self in an effort help them. But even then, as you know, most people are not listening to their High Self and are probably satisfied with themselves and the life they lead. Yet they may have ailments and ill-health that they accept as just being part of life and would be appalled to be told that they have brought the ill-health upon themselves by their attitudes and outlook.
I believe that one of the most corrosive emotions that can be buried deep within is resentment. This is buried anger and indignation that may even seem to have been resolved but is actually festering away below the surface, and while it exists we cannot be happy or at peace.

To examine this further, it is obvious that indignation refers to the fact that your dignity has been offended in some way. And it is easy to feel affronted especially if you are touchy and easily upset, but more often than not, such clashes are short lived and can be talked through. The really deep, destructive emotions are those that are long term, those you thought you had dealt with or brushed under the carpet. Perhaps there was someone in the past who gossiped about you in a malicious way. Or another suggested that you were incapable or would not come up to scratch in some respect. You may have lost your job or been passed over for promotion. It could be you felt offended because someone *refused* your help. Or perhaps you were even offended because someone *offered* you help, and you interpreted that as suggesting that you are foolish or inferior to them, and you felt deeply hurt.

You may have carried resentment all your life because of something that happened way back in childhood. Perhaps a parent left home and you felt abandoned, or another child seemed to be favoured. Or perhaps you felt unfairly blamed or punished for something you did not do. There are so many ways in which we can resent the way we have been treated, and in every case it is your Ego who is telling you that your dignity has been infringed and your Self challenged. This also means of course, that you have let your Ego take charge of your thoughts and emotions, and although it is trying to protect you, it is only bringing you deep seated unhappiness that is often the root of illness.

There really is only one way to deal with this and it is not easy because deep resentment can only be eradicated by true forgiveness, which initially might seem impossible. However, it can be done, firstly by realising and acknowledging that it is all in the past – it happened and no amount of bitterness or fretting can undo it. Furthermore, your Chattering Mind must not be allowed to drag you back into unwanted reminiscence where you relive the bad experience over and over again. Thirdly, it should be realised that the other person or people involved may be unaware of your resentment against them and may have completely forgotten the incident. You could be the only one suffering!

When once this is recognised you will start to think differently and look again at the circumstances that surrounded the cause of the trouble, and what pressures everyone was under at the time. This will help to clarify if you need to forgive yourself for the part you might have played, but whatever the circumstances, you will appreciate that there is now no need to carry bitterness forward. If a breach of trust was involved you obviously would not put yourself in the same position again, but otherwise you are capable of being generous and charitable, even knowing a wrong was done to you.

When you feel the time has come that you can really forgive, sit quietly as in meditation, or lie quietly in bed before you go to sleep, and send out Healing thoughts telling the person or others involved that you forgive them for what they did and that you no longer bear any grudge or enmity towards them. Tell them that you Bless them, that you are thinking kindly of them and that you are sending your very best wishes to them *as they are now*. If you can, surround them in a clear golden Light.

This will need to be repeated many times on successive days until you no longer feel any ill-will or hostility and your forgiveness will have registered deep within your subconscious. And there is no better feeling than having relieved yourself of the corrosion of resentment. If the Blessings are Heartfelt and spoken with truth and sincerity, you will realise that Divine Love is not an event or circumstance but a state of Being – your state of Being.

USING YOUR POWER
2018

Today I am going to talk about the part that you play in the powerful force that we call the Collective Consciousness of mankind. But perhaps before we get there it might be useful to recap some of the things we currently understand. For instance we understand that when the Earth changed its position in the Milky Way towards the end of the 20th century it involved a Shift that brought us under the influence of new powerful cosmic energies that were previously unknown to mankind.

Some of these energies come from our own Sun that for some years has been emitting flares of exceptional solar power. And this has been attracting a good deal of scientific interest in the hope that seismologists may be able to predict when flares will occur because, among other things, they have a big effect on our weather and global warming. Of course the Cosmic Shift hasn't only affected us, it has also affected all the other planets in the Solar System, although we don't as yet know what their reactions might be to the new energies now showering down upon us.

A prime example of how rapidly things are changing is how we lose track of time since it began to fluctuate. Some days it is hard to know what day of the week it is! But we are on the Fourth Bridge where Time is now converting from past, present and future into the Now – and those of you who have studied Mindfulness and living in the Now, know that when we can live every day to the full without fear of the future or regrets from the past, we can actually live in state of contentment and serenity. So I don't think we should be grumbling about how time is flying!

I am sure we all agree that we are living in extraordinary times and since I last spoke to you the political, social and technological changes in the world have been staggering. There are of course, still great inequalities between rich and poor, with the have-nots having less and less and the haves earning millions more than they can possibly need.

But unfortunately, we are now also witnessing political brinkmanship and sabre rattling between powerful national leaders, and there has been the obscene use of chemical warfare. Furthermore, we now see huge tented areas where of millions of displaced people are seeking refuge from bombing. It is an Exodus of historic proportions. But the die is cast and solutions must be found by the worlds leaders to deal with rogue states and find peaceful means of bringing mankind together for our common good.

You who are here today will have no trouble in recognising that human Ego is the root cause of war and always has been. It is either about gaining power or retaining power, gaining more land or gaining more property, or a perception of being superior to others because they are different in some way, or as we are seeing, extreme religious intolerance. Religious extremists do not understand that by beheading someone or setting off bombs in crowded places they create fear but they can't change the spiritual status of those killed. They will pass to the Higher Life with their same spiritual outlook and their eternal lives will continue as before.

The extremists' aim is to create fear and provoke us into a religious war by various acts of violence. But we must do all we peaceably can to resist the challenge. And that is why you and I are here. We may have forgotten, but we chose to incarnate at this particular time to assist in the Transition into the 5th Dimension. So let us look at how we go on from here.

In this group you are all healers who have devoted many years channelling Light, Love and Healing into the world's darkest places where it will help to change hearts and minds. You understand that it only takes one candle to bring light into a dark room and you have joined millions of other compassionate people and groups all working on the same healing frequency. These earnest appeals for peace and goodwill come from the four corners of the earth to combine together as a powerful force for good, and it is this Collective Consciousness that determines the overall state of humanity.

We are in an early stage of the Transformation and most of mankind is still governed by Third Dimensional beliefs that include material values and an insatiable desire for worldly goods. Additionally, millions of people who are dissatisfied with their lot are looking for 'change'. It is the magic word of the 21st century, the panacea for everything, but those who are ground down by ignorance, poverty, and oppression can only contribute to the Collective Consciousness by adding Fear on the one hand and vague Hope on the other.

And it is in this context that we should not overlook our own vulnerability. We need to remember that as we send Love and Compassion to the other side of the world to alleviate their sufferings, we ourselves are part of that same Collective Consciousness and are not immune from the effects of their fears, their anxieties and their negativity. Although, of course, we also profit from hope and other good thoughts that are issued elsewhere.

The world at this time is in turmoil and even we who know our purpose may at times wonder why it is necessary for certain distressing events to take place. But whether we like it or not, we are all involved in a great transformation in which there will be much upheaval, and at various times in the future it will become necessary for you to keep an open mind and try to understand new realities, and accept in trust things you can't understand. When you find it gets difficult for you, keep centred on your compassion for humanity - and your faith and insight will be your pillar of strength.

In my view it will be the atrocities and cruelties of this Fourth Dimension that will create even more widespread anxiety and fear, and will eventually will bring the nations together in a search for the security and wellbeing of all.

The good news is that mankind's Collective Consciousness is now being supplemented and enhanced by the higher spheres as the planet is being showered by waves of Love, and the Light of spiritual understanding, and its purpose is to bring about a state of equilibrium between the spiritual and the physical that is essential for life in the Fifth. And you are helping to create the conditions to bring this about.

It is all about how you live your life, and the vibrations you carry around that are picked up by all you meet. In this respect we all appreciate a smile, don't we, but we

might appreciate laughter even more. So don't neglect these very simple expressions of your personality as you can so easily bring sunshine into so many lives. You might think that in the overall scheme of things one person does not matter - but you do matter and you are powerful beyond your understanding. It is you and others like you who are holding up the collective state of humanity. So, my message to you today is – recognise and use your power.

You will find that under the new influences you will doubtless encounter unexpected changes in your own life and you may find yourself in difficult circumstances, but it is important to recognise that you have the power to control any feelings in yourself that are hurtful or upsetting.

It only takes the realisation of what is happening for you to stop what you are doing, and talking to your Guide firmly state aloud that you don't want to feel like this, and ask for it to be taken away. Standing or sitting quietly and breathing evenly, you will recognise that your Guide is near to you, and as you feel the warmth of his presence your unwanted feelings will just go away. In its place will be a calmness and a sense of wellbeing giving you the reassurance that spirit help is always accessible – you only have to ask, and believe, and it will happen. And then thank and Bless him.

Finally, the biggest boost to your spiritual progression is to frequently let your uppermost thoughts dwell on Gratitude for the many blessings in your life including those we tend to take for granted. Remember that the Universe always gives you more of what you send out and if your thoughts are of Gratitude you will receive more of what you are grateful for. And the more sincere and genuine the Gratitude the more of the same you will receive.

So think deeply and become aware of everything in life that supports you, and as you feel your heart swell with thankfulness, your perception of life and your perception of yourself will transform, and your Light will shine brighter than ever.

MEDITATIONS

MEDITATION – THE SACRED GARDEN
1990

Prepare for this meditation by wearing comfortable (not tight) clothes or belts. Do not lie on bed. Sit in a comfortable chair, upright if possible, put feet firmly on the ground and hands in your lap.
If your Chattering Mind intrudes turn your thoughts again to your breathing.

Forget everything external to yourself – leave all problems outside the room.
Start deep breathing. Listen only to your breath. Inhale and exhale slowly and deeply, and when you are ready visualise yourself standing in front of a beautiful royal blue velvet curtain. The colour is radiant and you gradually realise that the sheen radiating off the curtain is a powerful healing blue that you can breathe into yourself.

So breathe in the healing blue – feel it go down to the solar plexus, hold it briefly and with each breath exhale all the negatives within you. Breathe in the healing and exhale the anxieties, the anger, the restlessness, the fear, the indecisiveness, and breath out all that is worrying to you. Repeat this exercise several times until you feel relaxed and revitalised, ready to step through the curtain.

You find yourself standing inside a corridor. There are open doors on either side through which sunlight streams. But you focus on the end door facing you and are drawn towards it. You slowly walk down the corridor. When you reach the end door it opens automatically and you step out onto a lush, bright green meadow alive with all the most vibrant coloured wild flowers. Daisies, buttercups, celandines, mosses and pink clovers. The air is laden with their perfume.

Away to the right the meadow stretches as far as you can see. There is a copse of small trees and you know there are small squirrels and other friendly animals playing there. You look up and marvel at the clear blue sky

203

and you feel the gentle warmth of the sun, and you become aware of a blackbird's clear song. You are filled with peace from the song and the soft, warm breeze.

You do not walk to the right but look straight ahead to a small swift flowing stream that crosses your view. You go slightly down hill to the stream and look into the clear, sparkling water. You become aware of the colours of the pebbles under the clear, cool water, the glint of the sun on the tiny rivulets and the soft babbling sound of the flowing stream.

You choose to sit on the grass by the stream and let your fingers dangle in its waters. You do not feel alone, but you feel as a child, relishing being alone in utter peace and complete relaxation. You are happy, light-hearted, contented and know you have found something very precious.

You look up and realise that on the other side of the stream there is a hill and a path that stretches away into the distance. But you have no desire to explore this – you are in the right place, and you can sit in the warmth of the sun in perfect freedom and contentment until you decide to return or are called back by the person who may be controlling many of you meditating together.

When you return it is important that you completely retrace your steps – come back the way you went it – out through the corridor and back through the curtain. Sit quietly for a minute or two then open your eyes back in your room.

After a several meditations you may notice a bench in the meadow and decide that you would like to sit there. This will be good because it is where you will be meeting your Guide as you progress. But this is not to be forced or rushed and will happen naturally.

MEDITATION TO OPEN YOUR HEART
2014

This is a quiet meditation to open your heart to allow those in spirit who are guiding you, to come close. Sit comfortably with your feet firmly on the floor. Shrug your shoulders, relax your elbows, rest your hands in your lap, hold a crystal if you have one. Do not rest your head backward nor drop it forward. Breathe evenly and listen to your breathing. Sink deep into your seat. If during the meditation your Chattering Mind interrupts, go back to listening to your breathing

Here is your meditation. Think of yourself, the spirit you are and the life you are leading. Your normal state is one of contentment, but at this time you may have problems or wish things were different in some way. But pause, and think for a moment. Understand that whatever is happening is only a phase and that things <u>will</u> change.

What you require at this point in time is to understand that there is not anything that you <u>ought</u> to do, or nothing anyone we know, <u>ought</u> to do. If you do take action it will come from your thoughts, whether they come from the Ego or from your Higher Consciousness.

Do not concern yourself with "if only I had done so-and-so"– just accept yourself as you are NOW. Wherever you are now is only a stage in your life and development, and you will be moving on – if that is what you wish to do. Respect yourself knowing that you are trying to do your best with whatever you are faced with. And best is always good enough.

Remember that your Higher Self, of whom you are part, exists in a state of Love. So every time you are doing your best you are living as your Higher Self. So try and bring yourself to as high a frequency as you can and set a vibratory tone of Peace and Goodwill that will affect all who come within your orbit.

Relax. Sink deeply into your meditation. Breathe. Realise all the power that is coming to you from the Astral Plane. Open your heart to receive the peace that comes from the nearness of your Higher Self and send Love, Forgiveness or whatever is beneficial, to anyone you know who needs your tenderness at this time.

Remain in this peaceful state and note your impressions or feelings and come back to the room refreshed, calm and recharged with spiritual energy.

MEDITATION – HEALING RELATIONSHIPS
2014

At a recent meeting we explored how you could change another's negative or aggressive attitude by the way you treat them. At this stage of your development many frustrating people will cross your path and you will be tested, but however much they may try to upset you it will be up to you to bring calmness and harmony into the situation.

It can be difficult if you are caught unawares but often you will have a hunch that a meeting may not go smoothly and be prepared. The clue then is to meet with an open mind, without hostility on your part, and accept the person as he is, not allowing yourself to be dragged down into unhelpful argument or discussion.

On the contrary, if you are met with any kind of hostility, stand back, take a deep breath, open your heart and silently Bless that person and surround him with clear bright Light. It is through your desire for a better relationship that you will find the compassion and tolerance that allows you to send Love and Light into the situation.
This is often received by the other party as warmth and empathy, subtly affecting his attitude towards you.

Of course this is more than a physical exercise. The emotions involved here must be sincerely Heartfelt and are part of your own spiritual advancement. There is profound truth in the biblical saying, 'Give and ye shall receive' – more abundantly than you can possibly imagine.

So to heal a relationship begin your meditation by calling to mind someone with whom you have a less than perfect liaison and send the power of Light and Love to them. Visualise that person in a cocoon of Light and watch it get brighter and brighter as they are infused with the radiance of the Love you are sending. Hold this for as long as you wish and then Bless them when you leave.

You might follow that by visualising another person with whom you would like a better relationship, or who has a poor relationship with a third party, and as the Love and Light you can channel is inexhaustible, it will no problem to switch your thoughts and healing to that second person, or to both parties.

Always bring every part of your meditation to an end by Blessing the person(s) concerned so that you make a conclusive ending and come back from your meditation refreshed and fulfilled.

BIBLIOGRAPHY

THE JOURNEY HOME   Chris Thomas
LIVING IN THE NOW   Gina Lake
AWAKENING to the FIFTH DIMENSION   Vidya Frazier
A NEW EARTH   Eckart Tolle
SPIRITUAL GROWTH   Sanaya Roman
BEYOND RELIGION   Dalai Lama
THE FOOLS FIRST STEPS   Chris Thomas
LIFE BEFORE LIFE   Dr Jim B. Tucker
THE SEQUEL TO EVERYTHING   Chris Thomas & Diane Baker
OLD SOULS   Tom Shroder
THE SECRET   Rhonda Byrne
OPENING TO CHANNEL   Sanya Roman & Duane Packer
ONE HUNDRED ANSWERS   Gordon Smith
THE POWER OF NOW   Eckhart Tolle
WHERE REINCARNATION & BIOLOGY INTERSECT   Ian Stevenson
WELCOME HOME   Steve Rother & The Group
LIVING IN A MINDFUL UNIVERSE   Dr Eben Alexander & Karen Newell
RETURN TO LIFE   Dr Jim B. Tucker
FROM STRESS TO STILLNESS   Gina Lake

Printed in Great Britain
by Amazon